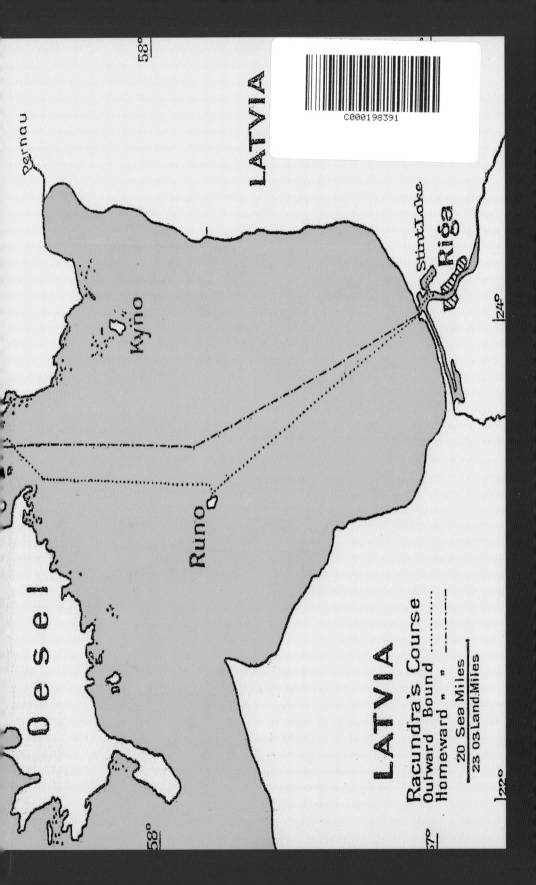

Racundra's First Cruise

The Arthur Ransome Society

The Arthur Ransome Society was founded in 1990 with the aim of promoting interest in Arthur Ransome and his books. For more information on the Society visit their website at www.arthur-ransome.org/ar

In 1997 members of the Society formed The Nancy Blackett Trust with the intention of purchasing and restoring one of Ransome's own yachts, the Nancy Blackett, and using her to inspire interest in the books and to encourage young people to take up sailing. She now visits many classic boat shows around the country.

To find out more about the trust, or to contribute to the upkeep of the Nancy Blackett please write to the Nancy Blackett Trust (reg. charity 1065058) at Sylvan Cottage, White House Walk, Farnham, Surrey, GU9 9AN or visit their website at www.nancyblackett.org

RACUNDRA'S FIRST CRUISE

by Arthur Ransome

Introduced and compiled
by Brian Hammett

Text and pictures © The Arthur Ransome Literary Estate
Introduction © Brian Hammett

This edition published 2003 by Fernhurst Books,
Duke's Path, High Street, Arundel, West Sussex, BN18 9AJ, England.

First edition published 1923 by George Allen & Unwin Ltd., London

British Library Cataloguing in Publication Data.
A catalogue record for this book is available from the British Library.

ISBN 1 898660 96 4

Printed in China through World Print.

Cover design by Simon Balley.

Artwork by Creative Byte.

For a free, full-colour brochure write, phone, fax or email us:

Fernhurst Books, Duke's Path, High Street,
Arundel, West Sussex BN18 9AJ, United Kingdom.
Phone: 01903 882277
Fax: 01903 882715
Email: sales@fernhurstbooks.co.uk
Website: www.fernhurstbooks.co.uk

CONTENTS

ARTHUR RANSOME, MASTER AND OWNER.

EVEGENIA SHELEPINA, COOK.

Aug 26. 1924

Racundra,
River Aa.

A man who owns a little ship
Must be forgiven many a slip
Committed when on shore.
A wife in every foreign port
Is unto him accounted naught;
And shall a book count more?

A borrowed book that's not at hand,
Being, for safety's sake, on land
Seems but a trivial slip;
As for your promised day in Heaven,
He's used to have his weekly seven
For Heaven is his ship.

But when at last his sails are furled
And he is once more in the world
Where little things count much,
An aeroplane with swiftest flight
Shall bear the book back to delight
It's owner's greedy clutch.

This poem was written during *Racundra's* third and last cruise under Ransome's ownership. Bridget Sanders, W. G. Collingswood's granddaughter, wrote in autumn 1997: "This poem was sent to Dr. John Rickman at 11 Kent Terrace, Regent's Park, London NW1, who must have been badgering AR for a book he had lent him. John Rickman was a distinguished psychoanalyst, and pupil of Freud's."

INTRODUCTION

"I ... took a deep breath and signed the contract. This was among the few wise things I have done in my life, for, more than anything else, this boat helped me to get back to my proper trade of writing."

Arthur Ransome (1884 – 1967), famous in later life as a children's author, wrote those words in 1922, having just committed himself to the building of his boat *Racundra*. The maiden voyage took place from 20th August 1922 until 26th September from Riga, in Latvia, to Helsingfors (Helsinki), in Finland, via the Moon Sound and Reval (Tallinn) in Estonia and back. On completion of the trip he wrote and published his first really successful book, *Racundra's First Cruise*.

I am delighted to have the opportunity to introduce a completely new edition of Ransome's first book on sailing. The original text of the first edition, of which only 1500 copies were printed, has been used in its entirety with the original layout. The original 30 photographs, and four sketch charts, are included together with more unpublished Ransome pictures and recent photographs of many of the places visited during the cruise.

The book has been out of print for many years; the last edition was a paperback published in 1984 by Century Publishers, London, and Hippocrene Books, New York, containing charts but no photographs. The story of how he came to write the book and his sailing activities in the Baltic in the early 1920s makes fascinating reading and tells us a great deal about the man and his approach to sailing and writing.

Ransome went to Russia in 1913 following an unsuccessful first marriage and having successfully defended a court case for libel, by Lord Alfred Douglas, over his book *Oscar Wilde, a Critical Study*, published in 1912. He had a desire to learn Russian and research and translate Russian fairy tales. His book *Old Peter's Russian Tales* was published in 1916. He was offered a job as a foreign correspondent and journalist by the *Daily News* and later the *Manchester Guardian*. He reported extensively on Russian matters, the First World War, and the aftermath of the October Revolution. Whilst in Russia he met and fell in love with Evgenia Shelepina, Trotsky's secretary. They lived together as lovers up until the time that Ivy, his first wife, agreed to a divorce. They married at the British consulate in Reval (Tallinn) on the 24th May 1924.

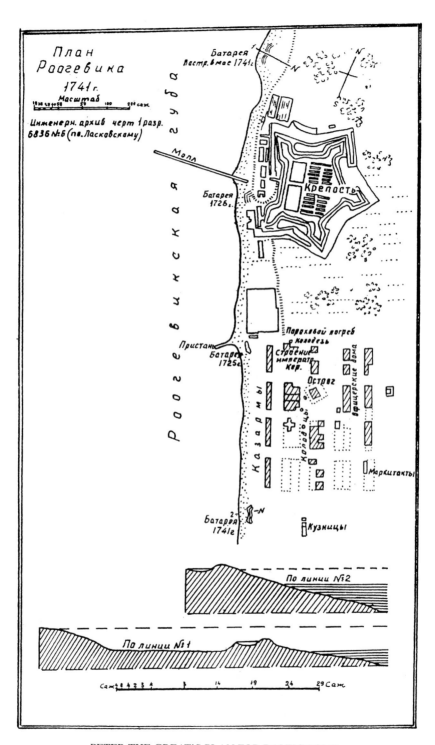

PETER THE GREAT'S PLAN FOR BALTIC PORT.

Ransome was a prolific writer and had already published 23 books by 1920. The most successful of his books were *Bohemia in London*, 1907, *A History of Story Telling*, 1909, and *Old Peter's Russian Tales*, 1916. He had also written two literary critical studies: one on Edgar Alan Poe, 1910, and another on Oscar Wilde, 1912. His life has been extremely well documented in his autobiography, his biography (by Hugh Brogan), and in other books by Christina Hardyment, Roger Wardale, Jeremy Swift and Peter Hunt. A literary society, the Arthur Ransome Society, TARS, is very active and his most famous boat *Nancy Blackett* (alias *Goblin*) is run by a charitable trust.

Having had a lifetime interest in Ransome's work, and having sailed in the Baltic in the year 2000 (where I used *Racundra's First Cruise* as a pilot book on several occasions), I was interested in discovering more about Ransome's Baltic sailing and to find out why and how he came to write *Racundra's First Cruise*. I was amazed by the accuracy of his description of *Racundra's* sailing area. The instructions for navigating the coasts of Latvia and Estonia, and in particular the Moon Sound, were as useful and accurate today as they were in the 1920s. The details of port and harbour entry and refuge anchorages also hold good today. Indeed, at one stage in our trip we "happened upon" Baltic Port (now called Paldiski North) whilst running for shelter from a southwesterly gale. We immediately recognised the description of the harbour. Once we had moored up the harbourmaster made us most welcome, told us that we could shelter for as long as we liked, at no charge, and even sent someone to sweep the quay where we had moored. This mirrored the treatment Ransome had experienced 78 years earlier. The harbourmaster and his colleague, the director of Paldiski Port, were very interested in the chapter *Old Baltic Port and New* in *Racundra's First Cruise* and, in exchange for a copy, gave us a pamphlet in Russian showing the original plans that Peter the Great had for the area. Ransome mentions on several occasions the uncompleted causeway and the old fort, both of which still exist today.

Ransome's background as an author and a journalist meant that, by nature, he was a compulsive writer. He kept diaries, logbooks, typed and handwritten notes and full details of his interests and activities. Most of this information still survives, mainly in the Brotherton Library at the University of Leeds.

Ransome's time in the Baltic up to 1920 had been fully occupied on journalistic activities and political writings of one sort or another although he was fiercely apolitical. In 1920 he and Evgenia had decided to live in Reval (Tallinn), Estonia, where he spent less time reporting and more time writing in-depth articles for the *Manchester Guardian*. This change of direction in his work activity meant that he was able to enjoy a little more free time to pursue his favourite pastime, fishing. Ransome had sailed a little on Coniston

Water, in the Lake District, with his friend Robin Collingwood, son of W.G. Collingwood (the Lakeland poet and writer, a father figure to Ransome after the death of his own father when Arthur was only 13). This introduction to sailing appears to have whetted his appetite for the sport, although in 1920 he considered himself very much a novice. However, he was to learn his skills very quickly.

To set the background for *Racundra* and *Racundra's First Cruise* it is important that we look briefly at his previous boats: *Slug* in 1920 and *Kittiwake* in 1921. This period of Ransome's life has been covered in his autobiography, published in 1976, and in his biography by Hugh Brogan, published in 1984. His early sailing is portrayed somewhat differently in his unpublished notes and writings. In looking at Ransome's work, shown in `American Typewriter` font, I have reproduced it exactly as originally written. In the 1920s many of the locations mentioned had different names and I have shown the current names in brackets.

In Peter Hunt's book *Approaching Arthur Ransome*, he criticises *Racundra's First Cruise* as "a curious volume: it is a specialist work, full of small details of what was a relatively uneventful cruise and many pages of minutiae of sailing and rigging and navigation, which are largely incomprehensible to the layperson. ... Ransome leavened the account of sailing in *Racundra* with encounters ashore, and possibly because they are padding and not focused on his dominant interest at the time, some are in the worst possible manner – pseudo-symbolic, inconsequential, and rather pretentious. (An example ... *The Ship and the Man*, first published in the *Manchester Guardian* in 1922). ... One of the features of *Racundra's First Cruise* is that it seems almost a sequel, or a book written for people intimately acquainted not just with sailing, but with Ransome's life. Old friends, in the form of boats as well as people, continually crop up, scarcely introduced. *Kittiwake* and *Slug* are referred to as though we knew them well."

This was possibly a justified criticism. However, by looking at Ransome's original material from 1920 and 1921 we can see how he came to include some of his previous experiences in *Racundra's First Cruise*.

SLUG

Ransome and Evgenia had moved to Reval (Tallinn) in 1919 and, after recovering from
a bout of illness (he suffered badly from stomach ulcers all his life), they moved to
Lodenzee in Lahepe Bay about 40 miles from Reval (Tallinn). Here they rented rooms
in a house with a quiet room where he could write. When shopping in Reval (Tallinn)
Ransome always strolled round the harbour looking for something with a mast and sail.
He recalls:

(Autobiography) In the end, walking one day along the beach, I came upon a man putting
a lick of green paint on a long, shallow boat with a cut-off transom that had once carried
an outboard motor. She had a mast. She was for sale. On the beach beside her were
large round boulders. I prodded her here and there and asked her price. The man named
a sum that sounded enormous in Esthonian marks but when translated into English

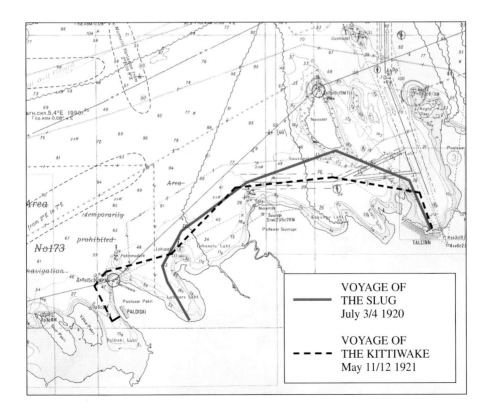

VOYAGE OF
THE SLUG
July 3/4 1920

VOYAGE OF
THE KITTIWAKE
May 11/12 1921

money came to something under ten pounds. The price included the boulders on the beach. ... I bought that boat. ... I found Evgenia, told her what I had done and said I would sail the boat from Reval to Lahepe next day. Evgenia, full of quite unjustified faith in me as a mariner, said that she was coming too.

The boat proved so slow that they christened her *Slug*. His autobiography chronicles in detail the maiden voyage to Lahepe Bay, including his diving overboard for a swim, and the difficulty he had getting back on board when the wind came up and *Slug* started sailing off to Finland with Evgenia in command. He was able with a superhuman effort to get back on board via the bowsprit, a feat that he was never able to repeat. The same trip is portrayed somewhat differently in his typewritten *Log of Slug*. He leaves out any mention of the difficulties of returning on board, an episode of which he was no doubt ashamed and wished to forget.

LOG OF THE SLUG

1920

6 a.m. Sunday July 3.

Dead calm. However, we packed our bags and went down to the pier, determined to get out of Reval no matter if only a little way, rather than postpone the start another day. At 6.30, though the water was like glass in the bay, there were occasional catspaws from the northwest. The scoundrel, who came to his pier head to see us off, said he was sure there would be wind of some sort, but the devil only could tell from what quarter. We hoisted sail, and had just enough wind to get us out past the bank of rocks that lies immediately north of the boat piers some few hundred yards from the land. Again dead calm. Thought of bathing from these rocks, but found them surrounded by piles, making approach impossible. Drifted. A very light wind from northwest filled our sail again, and we took a course north northwest. The wind was so slight and we moved so slowly that after tying a bottle to a rope and letting out astern, in case any gust should move her to unexpected hurry, I dived overboard and had a swim. Got on board again, and about seven thirty there was enough wind to give her yard or two of wake. We held on our course, the wind steadily getting a little stronger, till close inshore, north of the mill and south of the wooden pier at Miderando. We were passed by the two masted sailing boat which we had thought of buying the previous day. South of the pier we went about, and with a pleasant but very light wind

SLUG ON REVAL BEACH.

sailed west northwest making for the southern end of Nargon Island, a run of about eight and half a miles. With great delight we picked up the various buoys marked on our chart, and ran into the little bay southwest of the point, where we grounded the boat, landed, made a fire, and boiled up some cold tea. During the war, landing on Nargon was prohibited, and as we were not sure of our rights, we did not go as we had first intended to the village half a mile away to get milk, but lay low, and did not leave the shore. From where we made tea, we could just see the Surop lighthouse on the Esthonian coast.

Looking towards Reval, we saw a heavy black sky coming up from the east, and heard thunder. Presently the wind dropped to nothing. Then rose suddenly from the east, and we decided to lose no time, but to run for Surop, and try to get across before the worst of the storm should reach us, as we were on a beach exposed to the east, and could see nothing but rocky coast to the west. We got aboard at 4.30, and took a course southwest for the Surop lighthouse, thinking to shelter from the storm on the western side of Cape Ninamaa. But the storm was upon us before we were two miles on this slant of six. At least, not the storm but the wind. We had only a drop or two of rain, though the whole Esthonian coast east of Surop disappeared altogether in a dark cloud threaded by lightning. The sea turned black and then white in a moment, and the wind fairly lifted our little boat along, so that we were very grateful for the good stone ballast, which our scoundrel friend had stowed in her for the voyage. She stood it beautifully. And we were sorry for a much larger boat, beating up for Reval clear into the storm, which bowed her nearly flat to the water. The wind dropped as suddenly as it rose. The storm blotted out Nargon behind us, and passed, and we sailed slowly by Surop lighthouse, recognising it from our chart, as a white round tower surrounded by trees, at about seven o'clock.

From Cape Ninamaa, we took a course west southwest, hoping to pick up the Pakerort lighthouse about thirteen miles away. But the wind fell almost to nothing. It grew dark. At midnight, sailing, or rather drifting, only for a second or two at a time having any way on the boat, we learnt where we were, when the Pakerort lighthouse glittered out, and finding ourselves on a direct line between it and the Surop, we knew that we were not out of our course. To get home, we had only to round Cape Lohusaar into Lahepe Bay. But once before, fishing for sea-devils, I had been to the mouth of that bay, and knew that isolated rocks run out from Cape Lohusaar a considerable way into the sea. If there had been much wind, we should have run on close to the Pakerort, and then turned back on a southeast slant into the bay, which would have been safe enough. As it was there was not enough wind even to give one control over the boat, so there was nothing to do but to wait till dawn. It was a jolly dawn over the Baltic Sea and, as it lightened, we recognised Lohusaar Cape, only a mile or two before us, and with a slight wind from the southeast sailed past the rocks, which stood out even further than I had remembered across the bay. And then bearing up to the wind which was veering east southeast, cut into and across the bay. It was two in the morning when we were into the bay, and if the wind had held we should have been home to breakfast; but it fell away altogether. We made one interminable tack east northeast and anchored in an almost dead calm, bathed, made a tent out of the mainsail, and fell asleep like logs.

At eleven we woke, and found just enough wind to take us home to the southeast corner of the bay; where, after stripping, and towing her through the narrow channels in the sand banks, we anchored in shallow water, and came ashore, after having had a very good all round specimen of Baltic weather, and gained a very considerable confidence in "The Slug", besides a little in ourselves.

(Autobiography) It was a ridiculous beginning, to take an open boat for sixty miles of sailing, mostly tacking, along a coast we did not know, but it was not more ridiculous than some of our later experiments. Evgenia had never been in a sailing boat before, and I owe it alike to her ignorance and her courage that this first voyage did not in any way deter her from other adventures. We have never since been without some sort of boat, and for a number of years worked very hard to make ourselves reasonably efficient, taking every chance of sailing in vessels of every kind as well as in our own.

Two days after this eventful first trip Ransome drafted a letter to his old friend Barbara Collingwood (daughter of W.G. Collingwood), with whom he had been in love in his youth. The letter appears not to have been finished or ever sent. It does show, however, that Ransome was at an early stage in developing his sailing skills.

C/O British Consulate,
Reval.
July 5.1920.

My dear Barbara,

First voyage satisfactorily accomplished. I enclose with this a copy of the Log. The bit with the storm was exciting but short. If it had lasted longer, perhaps we should not have fared so well. As it was it greatly increased the belief I had in the boat and in myself, which, at the beginning, was extremely small. Before starting, we had to get a passport for the boat. They made me put E.P. down as "sailor". When we were starting, and leaving the pier to which we were tied up, she took an oar and backwatered instead of rowing by mistake, whereupon the scoundrel who sold us the boat remarked with a grin, "Your sailor does not know how to row". He had already in most uncomplimentary terms expressed his opinion of my own seamanship. I had to work entirely on what I remembered of Robin's instructions. But one thing he never taught me, and that was how to heave to in a wind and keep more or less in one place without handling the sails. I know the thing is done by fixing the sails and the tiller someway or other, but no amount of rule of thumb experiment arrived at the desired result. I shall be much obliged for detailed instructions, if possible with diagram on this point.

The rig of the boat is not quite the same as Swallow or Jamrach's. The gaff? (the stick at the top of the mainsail) projected in front of the mast. The boom is as per Swallow. There is also a triangular foresail (?) jib, called hereabouts the cleaver.

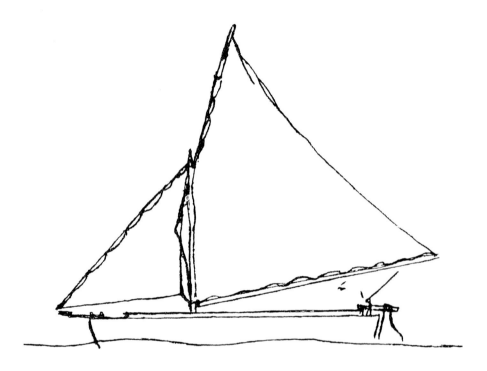

That is something like. She is I think 18 feet long. She was built about a hundred years ago, but she practically does not leak at all.

All her rigging is rotten. Ditto her sails, which are made of something suspiciously like old sheets. We've spent the day in repairs. In the course of the repairs arose about five hundred technical questions for Robin or Ernest, and neither of these Nesters are on hand. I have with trepidation but apparent success taken out the rope that howks the main sail up, and put it back t'other end on, because it had a knot at one place, which made it impossible to lower it altogether. Further I have developed what seems to me to be rather a shady trick of tying the low corner of the mainsail to the thwart beside the mast. Nothing else to tie it to. A screw with a ring to it probably meant for that purpose came out bodily, suggesting rottenness in the mast, which, for peace of mind, I have to refrain from investigating. E. has patched the mainsail with tablecloth, and talks of grey paint. She says she prefers boats to fishing, and has already learnt to sail the Slug in a calm. I think that unless some accident puts an end to our experiments, another month of Baltic cruising on a minute scale should bring us on a long way in the practical part of the business. But I fairly yearn for Robin, and curse every few minutes the many hours of possible sailing I missed at Coniston. I ought to have tied myself to Swallow, and slept on her, and gone out with her whenever Robin descended from on high to make her perform her mysteries. Then I should know a little more about it. I think I had better number every sentence in this letter, and beg for an expert commentary on each. It's the little things that I don't know, how on earth does one make a perfect circle of rope with no knot to fasten round (1) a hollow iron ring and (2) a pulley, by whipping it in the middle? How does one find except by a hundred very wearisome experiments how and where to fasten the rope that howks up the mainsail to the infernally awkward bit of stick that goes across the top of the same instead of ending with jaws round it like the similar stick in good old Swallow?

The Baltic, I may say, has one great advantage over our own in that there is no tide. So if you hit a sandbank with your keel once, you can be sure of hitting it again at any hour of the day. Rocks do not play bo-peep with you. There are hundreds and thousands of them but where they are there they remain, and the wise sailor takes off his hat to them as he passes.

I have got a pretty good German chart of 1908, showing the whole of the gulf of Finland, from Hango in Finland, and the island of Worms (Esthonian) right up to Petrograd, on a scale of what I make out to be about $6^{1}/_{4}$ miles to the inch. It gives inset charts of the approaches to the principal harbours, on a scale little more than twice as big. It has little miniature pictures of all the lighthouses, so that you can recognise them by day. Enormous fun. I have now made the acquaintance of four of them.

The awful thing about open boat cruising is that one gets absolutely no rest. There is no cabin, no means of sleeping out of the sun, and for grub one has either to land, an unwelcome and risky operation, or else do without a fire and exist on sandwiches. I have absolutely made up my mind to get a boat for single-handed sailing with a cabin, and with everything thought out wilily to make her working easy. Ratchet reefing for example. Everything fixed for comfort so that one could really live on board, which in an open boat like the Slug is impossible. On our thirty-six hour trip, I had only four hours of v. uncomfortable sleep in the bottom of the boat, while at anchor.

Now please, if possible, get answers to some of the questions in this letter... particularly about heaving to. I know that by some trick it is possible to fix up the boat so that she will look after herself, and leave you free, for example to mend a rope, or to eat a meal.

The only known photograph of *Slug*, with Evgenia standing on board, was taken on the beach at Reval (Tallinn), shortly after the purchase of the boat. The authenticity of this photograph is born out by the sketch in Ransome's letter. Photographs attributed to *Slug* in several publications, including his autobiography (published nine years after his death) are in fact of Ransome's third boat, the sailing/fishing dinghy, built in Riga, Latvia in late 1921. The description of this boat with a fish box built around the centreboard case gives a positive identification. There was no fish box in *Slug*.

(Autobiography) I will say no more of *Slug*, ill-fated boat. Lahepe Bay was not a very good place in which to keep her afloat. We could reach her only by swimming, and get ashore only by deep wading after bringing her in. We used a raft as a dinghy and it had a bad habit of tipping us sideways into the water. *Slug* twice sank at her moorings. Once we left her snugly at anchor and came down to the shore again to find that her mainsail had been stolen.... We had a lot of fun with *Slug* and the raft, but knew that she was only a makeshift. Our walls were covered with Baltic charts and the plans of boats, and I was able to sweep the worries of writing about Russia out of my head by teaching myself the elements of navigation.

He was so affected by the loss of *Slug's* mainsail that he typed an essay on the subject:

Moral Reflections on Theft

There are degrees in robbery. Some thefts are worse than others. I am prepared to forgive natural thefts such as cherry-stealing, in which boys are no worse than chaffinches, and, however they may hurt the pocket, do not grievously offend the moral sense. The theft of money is more sordid, contaminated as it is by the least uplifting of human interests, but it has a practical, sensible character, and can often be justified. It is an evil involved in an imperfect system of distribution. The theft of a fountain pen comes nearer sin. It can never be to the thief the intimate thing that it was to its owner. The gain of the thief is less than the loss occasioned to the owner. The theft of clothes may or may not belong to the some category. The theft of new clothes, if they fit the thief I find easily forgivable, at any rate more easily forgivable than, for example, the abduction of a worn old shooting coat in which every rent and patch is as it were a notch on the tally stick like an entry in the diary of the owner's life. Horas non numero nisi serenas, is as true of the patches in a shooting coat as of the moving shadow of the sundial. Similarly, I find the theft of a fishing rod far worse than the appropriation of any quantity of mere hooks and similar tackle. The quality of book stealing depends entirely on the personal characters of the thief and the sufferer. I have myself on one on two occasions stolen books, committing crimes for which if there is to be a summing up and general judgment day I confidently hope to be forgiven. And once at least in stealing a book from a man who never read it but owned it merely as a sort of filthy ostentation, I performed an act for which, if there is justice in heaven I expect not forgiveness but reward.

But if the theft of a book may be an act of virtue there are other thefts as black as murder, no; blacker, like the theft of a man's soul. The theft of a cripple's wooden leg is a deed whose ugliness will be pretty generally admitted, since, reducing him to immobility, inflicting on him paralysis, it is a particularly vile kind of assault. But even that is not so vile a crime as that which is still ruining the world for me, stopping the cruise of the Slug almost in its auspicious outset. Next to the theft of a man's soul, I can think of no villainy so utterly abominable as the stealing of the mainsail of a little ship. And that, unthinkable as it must be to any honest man, loathsome to any sailor, actually occurred, on the night between July 7 and 8, in Lahepe Bay, in Esthonia.

Now the mainsail of a little ship is her very soul. Take it away, and you take away the thing that distinguishes her from mere water carriages propelled by oars or steam or petrol. Removing it, you remove the thing that links her with the wind, with the seagulls she resembles. You commit worse than murder. You take the very soul out of her and leave her a dead thing.

It was not a new sail. We had spent the whole of July 6 in patching it with bits of tablecloth. Five laborious patches we had put it. Nor was it a good sail, but made of some inexpensive material, intended, I believe for the underclothing of the Russian army. But, patched and cheap as it was, it was wing enough to lift her through the blue waters of the Baltic Sea, and indeed, like a great wing, towered proudly above her stumpy mast, curving away wing-like to the end of her long boom.

I had left her, with her foresail neatly gathered about her bowsprit, and the great mainsail wrapped about boom and gaff, and laced with the main-sheet, as neat as a fop's umbrella in repose. She rode to a buoy, improvised during the morning. I had sunk a sugar case with wire rings at the top corners, from which wires meeting in the middle were fastened to a twisted wire rope. With terrific labour, sweating in the sun, I had dragged heavy stones out to sea. Struggling under water, I had done diver's work, and planted them one by one in the sugar case. To the end of the wire rope I had fastened a little barrel. I had taken her a little trip to try certain small improvements in rigging, and we had returned, tied up to our own buoy, in itself a satisfaction, and swum ashore, stopping again and again, as we walked from the beach, for the pleasure of seeing her there swinging so pretty, with her head under her wing, like a seagull resting for the night, with the blue bay opening out behind her, and the sun setting away in the north behind the Baltic Sea.

And then, in the morning, I had stayed at home and worked, my mind, none the less, caressing her. Women came up from the shore, and told me, in answer to my questions, that she lay there all right. At last, after luncheon, I took the tiller on my shoulder and set out for the shore. To get to the shore, you have to cross a wide strip of sand with glaucous coloured sharp edged and sharp pointed grass, and, at the very edge of the sea there is a raised bank, so that the little ship is not visible until you are actually within a few feet of the water. The moment I stood on the bank, I knew that something was wrong. The boom was lying flat, not cocked up perkily as I had left it. I thought that boys had been on board and meddling with the ropes. When I caught the sunlight on the boom, and saw instead of sail, bare wood, I could not believe it. We swam off. The wind was from the land, and the water had turned very cold in the night, but not so cold as our hopes, which, until that moment had been at boiling point, thinking that next day we should continue our cruise, and round the Pakerort lighthouse, and away by Baltic Port and Odensholm, for Hapsal and the Island of Dago.

We clambered on board, to the last minute thinking that perhaps some imp of mischief had taken off the sail, and stowed it in the forecastle. To the last minute I could not believe that any man could be so vile. But, as I tumbled in over the stern, my hopes and my faith in humanity fell together like plummets, and I knew the worst. The boat was strewn with little scraps of rope, clean cut with a knife. The thief had simply cut all that impeded him, and left the boom, bare, stripped among the wreckage.

KITTIWAKE

In the spring of the following year – 1921 – Ransome purchased his second boat *Kittiwake,* smaller than *Slug* but with a small cabin.

(Autobiography) The *Slug* had whetted our appetite for a better boat, one with a cabin. Wandering round the harbour we saw one which we decided would take us as far as the little harbour of Baltic Port where we planned to spend the summer. With a timely windfall from an American paper we bought her and called her *Kittiwake* because we liked the picture of that gull in Coward's bird-book and imagined we were the first to think of it. Later we found that a great many other people had the same idea and that there were flocks of *Kittiwakes* in English waters. She was a bit of a joke really, sixteen foot long overall with a beam of six foot and a draught of five, her normal keel having been deepened by a rather flimsy addition. With such a deep draught we needed a dinghy for getting ashore, but there was no boat builder in Reval to make one. Eventually I found a firm of undertakers and pointed out to them that if they could make coffins they could make dinghies. They agreed to try and a few days later produced a triangular box looking like the bows of a boat sawn off square by the first thwart. There never was such a boat for capsizing. If I shifted my pipe from one side of my mouth to the other I never knew what might happen. However, there it was, a dinghy, better than nothing. We fitted out *Kittiwake* with mattresses for her two horribly narrow bunks, orange curtains for her miniature portholes, a primus, a kettle, a saucepan, a frying pan, a couple of plates, a couple of mugs, knives, forks, spoons, and were ready for sea.

In April 1921 Ransome recalls the finding of *Kittiwake* in a typewritten article:

The Boat

Captain Jackson of the steamship "Cato" had steamed into Reval on the Saturday, bringing with him the news that he had been unable to buy us the double ended lifeboat which he was to have brought out to be decked and sparred here and turned into a shallow draft cruising yacht particularly fitted for the voyages we had in mind. It was a sunny March day, and, bearing up under this disappointment, E and I were walking along Fisherman's beach, making up our mind to go at once to the island of Oesel and there build a boat. All along the beach were open boats,

FITTING OUT KITTIWAKE.

bottom up, disreputable old yachts sheltered from the weather by scraps of rusty tin plate or boards, other old yachts which their despairing owners had abandoned to the full devilry of the winter, realising that no amount of protection would save them from the damage they had already received. We found a double ended fishing boat, decked, with a cabin forward, in good condition except for the rudder fastenings, one of which had rusted away. The rascal who owned her was hanging about, and offered her for sale for 65,000 Esthonian marks (£65) explaining that he had carried apples in her, and that she would be a good boat for smuggling. We looked her all over, and decided that with a lot of changes she could at a pinch be made fit for our plans, but we had not £65 to throw away on a boat not worth a quarter of that amount. We walked on, to the little harbour of the fishing boats, where two or three fishing boats, with spritsails, were making ready for sea. An old fisherman with a brown bottle prominent in his breast pocket was lolling in the stern of one of them. A small boy and a serious sister aged about nine brought him a basket of provisions. A couple of stout young men dropped over the wooden pier into the open boat and pushed off, punting her to the mouth of the shallow harbour, and then set their sprit across the sail while the old man with the bottle held the main sheet and steered her through the opening in the breakwater. The light wind from the land caught her, and effortless, she rippled away over the almost smooth bright blue water of the bay. It was unbearable to think that, since we had failed in getting a boat from England, we were likely to loose the best months of the year in watching other folks sail away while we plodded grimly from boat-builder to boat-builder on the shore.

There were more boats, beyond the little harbour, and, though it was teatime, and we had already made up our minds that we had not the smallest chance of finding what we wanted, we decided just to walk along and look at what there was. This part of the beach was deserted. The boats lying higgledy-piggledy were mostly wrecks. It was scarcely worthwhile to walk further. However, we picked our way over half melting ice and stinking seaweed, which had been preserved in ice throughout the winter in order to pollute the spring. Here and there where the ice had melted the seaweed gave way between us, and we stepped ankle-deep in slush. We had just made up our minds to go back when we came upon a spectacle that would have been surprising in any other country.

A young man in the tunic, boots and breeches of a cavalry officer, but with a cap that showed that he belonged to the mercantile marine, was sitting on a stone scraping barnacles from the bottom of a stout dumpy little yacht lying on her beam ends on a patch of sand. The little yacht was carvel built, in Finland, as we afterwards learnt. In these parts they invariably spoil clinker built boats by using planks too wide for the purpose, which presently fall apart. The little yacht had a bluntish nose and a stern obviously built for comfort rather than for speed. She had a cabin, quite extraordinarily roomy for her diminutive size.

He decided to purchase the boat and his handwritten notes describes his first trip after having paid the deposit.

April 13

The owner, who was going off to Zoksa to superintend the docking of a little steamer, proposed to take Kittiwake round to the Yacht Club in the harbour. He collected a stout lad with a leaky dinghy, and sent me off in the yacht. I found that though the ballast was on board the floorboards

KITTIWAKE AT REVAL.

were not, and it was easy to see that the ballast was very badly laid, many of the heavy pieces resting actually on the bottom boards. Presently the dinghy arrived again with the owner, the boy, and the carpenter who was said to have begun making the pump, but had actually come to take preliminary measurements.

I as purchaser, not having yet taken possession, refrained from taking responsible part in the proceedings of making sail and getting away. The owner and the boy worked together, the boy shinning up the mast to reeve the jib halyard. It was very gusty, one squall following another from the shore. The wind being from the land, there were no waves. Still it was a goodish day in which to test her, and my doubts as to her top heaviness were confirmed when I heard the owner, wildly battling with the hanking of the jib on the forestay, remark, "We shall have to put a couple of reefs in the mainsail."

We got off without incident, and sailed round the harbour; even with two reefs down she sailed with the water on her deck and under her coamings, we had to luff up to every extra bit of squall. She heeled over at such an angle that it was impossible to sit in the cockpit. At least sitting in it, one felt as if one was in the pouch of a catapult, which at any moment might project one violently into the sea. One had to get outside and perch on the weather coaming or lean on the hatchway. That of course was the penalty for having so delightful a cabin.

We went about and sailed east round to the new harbour. She made a very fair pace. She manoeuvred beautifully, but was a bit of a handful running before the wind, having a distinct tendency to spin one way or the other, and to execute one jibe after another. This of course was partly due to the squally wind, coming from behind the rain, and shifting every minute. Going about with her, however, was a treat. She was on with the new tack before she was off the old, with a joyful flick of her skirts. I felt she was a good deal too skittish a temperament for me, but decided that if I survived two months of her methods of education I should be fit to sail any boat and to survive.

At last we sailed back to our starting point and then along the shore to the harbour, turned around with the wind behind us, and then into the harbour, tacking up into the opening between the moles. We sailed along quickly into the harbour and found that the only available buoy was tucked away under the combined stems of a tug and a big sailing barge. I remarked rather tentatively, in my capacity as passenger, that he had brought no oars, and no anchor chain, only a short length for tying up to a buoy. "We shall not need them," he replied. "We can get to our moorings." Instead of waiting to be helped by someone in a dinghy who afterwards enjoyed his discomfiture, he tried to pick up the buoy in this impossible position; with the natural result that he carried away his bowsprit (oak) broke his bobstay (wire rope) and half the strands of one of the port shrouds. Your purchaser lent and reached our moorings with considerable emphasis.

(Autobiography) For practice we started taking her out of harbour every day. She was top-heavy and heeled over to her cabin-top even with two reefs down and we had to steady her with scrap-iron ballast, hoping wishfully that she would learn good manners. But we lost faith rapidly, and this made us more and more determined to have a really good boat, big and comfortable to live on board for months on end and fit to be sailed to England if and when we wanted to do so.

Two days after *Kittiwake's* first sail Ransome and Evgenia met Otto Eggers, a well-

COFFIN MAKER'S DINGHY.

known German designer and boat builder of racing craft who had a large boatyard in Reval (Tallinn) before the First World War. Estonia's new nationalism had left him without a yard, but still designing.

(Diary 1921)
15 April

In the evening went and fell in love with Mr. Eggers, with the probable result that we shall have a boat built by him. The enthusiasm of the fellow when he is talking of a possible boat simply carries me off my feet and hundreds of pounds out of my depth. He proposes a perfect boat to go anywhere single-handed with every kind of tweak. Talked it over with Evgenia who herself is bowled over by Eggers. She too votes for getting his boat.

21 April
Evgenia says she can live until April 21, 1923 with no new clothes?!!!!

In May the dinghy that had been ordered from the local undertaker arrived.

4 May

Dinghy arrived. Complete failure.
Evgenia refuses even to try it, or to be rowed in it, or to take it with us
so it may be regarded as 11,000 wasted Esthonian marks, and we are still
without a dinghy and should be starting. (In Evgenia's hand:) Evgenia herself
is a complete failure (In Arthur's hand) Only partial.

On May 11 the Ransomes' undertook their first major voyage in *Kittiwake*
to take the boat from Reval (Tallinn) to Baltic Port (Paldiski North), a more
convenient place to keep and sail the boat during the summer and a lot nearer to their
lodgings at Lodenzee. He typed an article detailing the trip:

REVAL TO BALTIC PORT

In the evening of May 10 we dined on the Esthonian ship "Kalevipoeg"
which was leaving for Stockholm the next day, and after dinner went on
board the Kittiwake and made all ready for a start before turning in. Our
one portmanteau filled the whole space between the bunks, and were so
narrow that lying on our backs we projected on one side into the luggage
and on the other pressed hard against the sides of the boat. It was a clear
night of stars and the barometer was steady. We hoped to get away at
dawn but this was our first night on board, and we found it quite
impossible to get to sleep until something like one in the morning. The
alarm clock broke into abrupt song at three a.m. We disregarded it and
slept on until about half past six when there was a heavy bump, followed
by impatient hammering on the cabin roof. I extricated my feet from
under the after deck, doubled forward like a snake and looked out of the
cabin door to find two Esthonians in a dinghy alongside.

"Good morning," said one of them. "We have just got in from Loksa.
It's a fine wind. Come on with us and sail together to Baltic Port."

"Have you got any vodka?" said the second, who had evidently drunk all
he had, and had had a considerable quantity.

"We are talking about something else," said the first.

I craned over the cabin roof to see their boat, and saw that she was at least twice as big as the Kittiwake, and said that though we were going to Baltic Port we could not expect to keep up with them.

"Have you got any vodka?" said the second again.

"Choose a more reasonable moment," said his companion.

"But, if we have not got enough vodka ourselves…"

His companion disregarded him, said we should meet at Baltic Port and pushed off. They rowed quarrelling to their yacht, and we never saw them again.

However, they had done their work in calling us, and indeed there was a pleasant wind blowing from the south off the land, which should have carried us very comfortably out of the deep bay. So we set about dressing. Now dressing for two in a cabin not large enough for one, encumbered by a lamp that seems as big as an arc light and as active as a football, with the whole space between the bunks packed with oars, boathook, the oars and mast of the dinghy, a kitbag and a portmanteau, not to speak of a Primus stove, with its threatening little roar of fire hotting up our coffee is not an operation that can be performed with speed. It was actually seven thirty before we were setting the mainsail and eight before we had the anchor up, and with the oars were slowly pulling out of the harbour.

I moved Kittiwake with the oars, for the wind had dropped, and I could have seen to shave in the water of the harbour. The old man who looks after the Yacht Club shouted to ask if we had written our destination in the book for that purpose. I told him we had not, and that with a dead calm it was likely that we should have no destination at all. At nine we were drifting outside the harbour, and decided that in any case we would spend the day on the water. There was no wind where we were, but the water was ruffled further out, and the smoke from the tall factory chimneys had an encouraging unanimity. The air was stirring and presently our sails filled, rather half heartedly, and we had steerageway. In about an hour's time we had reached the boom that lies off the breakwater on Karlo Island. At this point the wind, such as it was, swung round to the N.N.W. It was just enough to keep us moving.

Reval some two sea miles away lifted its castle rock, its tall thin spires and towers, and the monstrous gold-domed Russian church breaking with a strange exotic touch of Byzantium the Gothic and Scandinavian outlines of the place. Few towns are more beautiful from the sea. The coastline on either side is low and the great rock lifted from the sea is from a distance almost like an island. From where we lay and drifted we could see the low shore of the bay curling round and out to sea, to the island of Wulf, low on the northern skyline. Far away we could see the landmarks, the white house on the shore and the triangular ruined end of the Briggitten monastery. To the northwest was the long low island Nargon, with the lighthouse on its northernmost point, just visible in the mist.

We were wondering if we had any chance of losing sight of Reval that day, but decided at least to get as far as the point before turning back. With the wind in its present position we had to fetch away again before attempting the point, which we did and by noon were off the second promontory of Karlo.

We kept moving, but no more, and had to throw matches overboard to convince ourselves that we were not really standing still. We calculated that we were making something well under a mile an hour. I thought of anchoring under Nargon for the night, but thought it better to keep on, as my chart was not in sufficient detail to show the way into the anchorage there, though it showed clearly that there were plenty of rocks along the shore, and I remembered that the Kittiwake drew five feet, so that I could not simply beach her, as I was able to do with the Slug the year before.

At teatime we were between Nargon and Surop, in the place where last year, on just such a clam day, we had had to fight our way across to shelter in a squall that gave us all we wanted and a little more. Through the binoculars, we saw the Kalevipoeg which had left Reval at two, standing out to sea. We could already see the two lighthouses on Surop. One conical, low on the shore, and the other, shoulder high in trees standing on the rising ground of the promontory.

E. set the Primus going in the cockpit, and filled the thermos with hot water for the evening's grog, for it was now clear that we should spend the night at sea. We made a good meal at the same time, of cheese, bread and butter, sardines, beer and biscuits. I did not feel altogether happy, because the barometer now began to move down, and calms on the Baltic are nearly always broken by unpleasant weather. Also, we now had nowhere to take shelter until we made Lahepe Bay, with its awkward entrance from the east, or finished our journey by rounding the precipitous point of Pakerort.

We drifted on, and the sun set in a low bank of darkish clouds. Rags and tatters of cloud appeared as if from nowhere overhead, and yet what with the little wind, and the drag of our abominable dinghy, let alone the sturdy build of the Kittiwake, we hardly moved at all. At eleven p.m. we were close off Surop. It now became quite dark. The moon disappeared behind clouds and the wind strengthened a little from the northwest, though not enough to account for the swell from the same direction, which, together with the falling barometer made me sure that a blow was coming from the same direction.

A perfectly horrible three hours followed, during which I had to steer by the lights of Surop and Nargon, now and again catching a faint glimmer of the Pakerort lighthouse far ahead, and making our way slowly past the light buoy northwest of Surop, and so towards Lohusaar point, the rocks of which I had had good opportunity of observing last year. I did not want to lose any opportunity of getting along, because I was certain that the weather was on the point of changing.

When at last the sun came up through a cage of thin bars of cloud we found we were quite near Lohusaar, and could see the immense crowd of seabirds on the rocky islands near the point, and hear our first cuckoo of this year calling in the woods on the shore. Thirty yards from us a seal was puffing and blowing. The barometer had now fallen a full tenth, and the swell from the N.W. had markedly increased. I drank a glass of coffee (my teeth were chattering after sitting at the tiller all night) made a short tack out to sea and then setting a course that would take us comfortable clear of Pakerort, gave the tiller to E., and had half an hour's rest in the cabin.

A little after six the wind freshened, and for the first time we began to move at a respectable pace, but with the wind the sea got up and the Kittiwake, though she lifted her nose fairly well, none the less was stopped almost dead at each considerable wave, so that we had not anything like the pace we should have had. We got across the mouth of Lahepe Bay and for the first time saw Pakerort near. Red cliffs, sheer down to the water's edge, a tall slim

KITTIWAKE AT BALTIC PORT.

lighthouse on the point, the very sight of it put fresh heart into us for we knew we had only to round it to get between Pakerort and the Roogo islands, and to find our harbour, which lies along the western side of the point. Still, the wind was extremely strong and, the waves stopping the poor Kittiwake almost dead at each blow, I began to be afraid we should not weather the point without another tack to sea. However, the wind obligingly shifted a degree or two northwards and at 8 a.m. we passed just inside the first buoy off the lighthouse, at 8.25 passed the second and, a minute later, let out the mainsheet and steered southward running about half a mile off the shore to avoid a reef which projects just north of the harbour. The wind and waves were now on our starboard quarter, and I had my work cut out to bring the bigger waves right aft one after another so as not to give them a chance of spinning us round broadside on, as they very clearly longed to do. They hurled the dinghy first one side, then the other, now broadside on, now charging down upon us like a battering ram. I hauled in the dinghy's painter bringing her nose as near as I could, so that she could not get much momentum for her blows. But there was so much wind that I could not leave the tiller to fix a fender, and the dinghy hit our counter with the regularity of a steam hammer and seemingly nearly as hard, whenever the waves did not do worse with her and, lifting her bodily, threw her nose actually over the counter and seemed likely to bring her bodily on board.

Before passing the boom on the end of the reef and turning southeast for the harbour mouth, I went about in a smooth patch, to avoid jibing in such a sea when my steering was still further hampered by the dinghy. The Kittiwake in spite of all her handicaps accomplished this satisfactorily, and at 9 a.m. we were rushing before the wind down to the entrance of the port, where we had already seen the red funnel of the Cato, a British steamship and a friend of ours, which had left Reval a day or two before. We rounded the entrance, and met a strong puff of wind through the narrow passage, made still narrower by the Cato's tall block stern towering above us. We had not room to tack, so, very clumsily, and tired out, we hauled down our sails, fought up against the wind inch by inch with the oars and, finally catching a rope's end flung from the Cato, were towed along her sides and made fast after a twenty five hour passage.

Arthur and Evgenia sailed *Kittiwake* in and around Baltic Port (Paldiski North) throughout June and July, often taking trips to the Roogö (Pakri) islands, one of their favourite places for picnics. He recorded each day's sailing events in his diary. They often sailed with their friend Leslie, at that time British Consul in Reval (Tallinn). When Grove, Leslie's successor, married them, Leslie, unable to be present, left a bottle of champagne for them in his room upstairs. Ransome's diary also records that they sailed with another friend, this time from Riga, referred to as the Kaiserwald Wizard. The diary confirms the comment in his biography about sailing in other boats. Ransome's description of the island of Little Roogö (Vaike Pakri) in *Racundra's First Cruise* tells us that he was very familiar with this particular island. His log records several trips there and back from Baltic Port (Paldiski North). In the early nineties Andres Tonisson, an Estonian scientist, visited the islands. He produced a sketch map showing the route Ransome described. Readers of the book *Peter Duck* will notice a very strong resemblance to the fictional Crab Island.

In August 1921 the Ransomes moved to Riga in Latvia and Arthur acquired his third boat, a sailing/fishing dinghy. From photographs of the boat the design is very similar to plans for a sailing dinghy drawn by Otto Eggers whilst he was designing *Racundra*. Egger's dinghy is however smaller, only 2.5 metres long, and without a centreboard and is more likely to be the dinghy shown on board *Racundra* in the illustrations in *Racundra's First Cruise*. The plans for this dinghy are with Ransome's

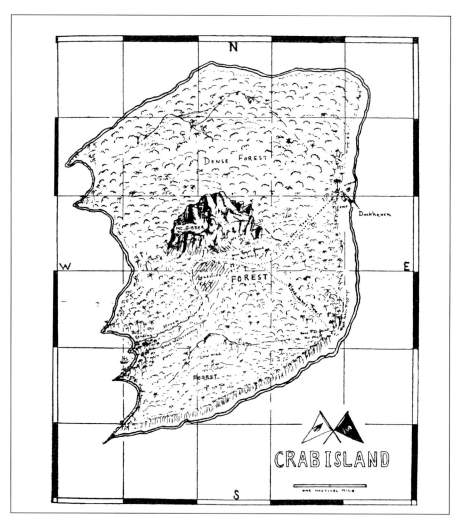

CRAB ISLAND IN "PETER DUCK".

papers in the Brotherton Library. The Latvian dinghy may well have been built using a modification of these plans.

His autobiography continues:

This happy summer based on Baltic Port ended half way through August when we moved our headquarters to Latvia. We rented rooms in a small house in Kaiserwald, outside Riga, on the shores of Stint See, a pleasant lake beside the forest. A Lettish boat-builder made me, in a few days, a small boat for fishing and sailing with a fish box

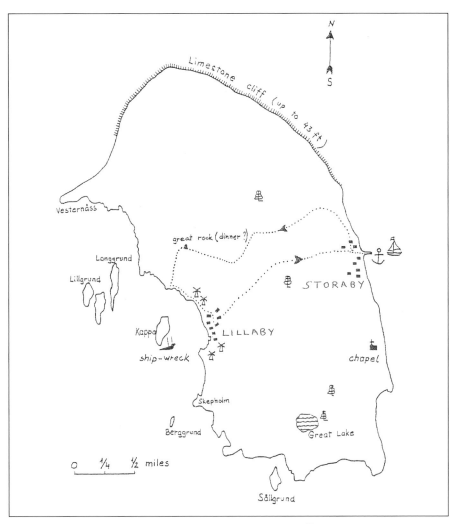

THE ISLAND OF LITTLE ROOGÖ.

built round the centreboard case and a small leg-of-mutton sail.

I liked the little fishing dinghy well enough to think it possible that the Riga boat-builder could translate my dream ship (on whose design Eggers had been working while I was in Russia) from paper into fact. The man had built an eight-tonner and was confident that he could build my boat. I went to Reval, talked it over with Eggers, came back with the preliminary drawings, showed them to the builder and, before leaving for England, took a deep breath and signed the contract, determined one way or another to do enough writing to pay for it.

EVGENIA AND ARTHUR ON LITTLE ROOGÖ.

EVGENIA AND LESLIE ON LITTLE ROOGÖ.

RACUNDRA

Ever since Ransome moved to Estonia he had at the back of his mind been considering writing a book. In a letter to his mother he mentions the possibility:

To Edith R. Ransome

January 19 1921
Reval

My dearest Mother

Very many thanks for the sailing book...
... The Esthonian book is a sheer luxury, because I cannot hope to make a penny out of it. People won't read a serious book on Esthonia. The only hope of making them read it is to make it a jolly sort of travel book, with lots of camping and fishing and sailing shoved in...

... I have got a publisher for the Esthonian book; at least I think so, but as I have already remarked, I shall make no money out it, lucky if it pays for the boat....

.... Could you buy "The Falcon on the Baltic" by E.F. Knight, 3/6 and send it. You can get it from G. Wilson, 23 Sherwood St., Piccadilly Circus, W.

With much love,

Your affectionate and now thoroughly middle-aged son.

Arthur

Following the Ransome's move to Riga in the autumn of 1921 their sailing activities were limited to the new sailing/fishing dinghy. No further mention is made of *Kittiwake* in Ransome's papers, presumably left or disposed of in Baltic Port

(Paldiski North). However in *Racundra's First Cruise* he reports seeing her in Reval (Tallinn). "… *Kittiwake* herself, unkempt, dilapidated, lovable little thing, was moored just the other side of the mole."

The building of *Racundra* is briefly described in the opening chapter of *Racundra's First Cruise*. He talks about the building in his autobiography:

Meanwhile *Racundra* was being built in a wooden shed on an island near the mouth of the Dvina River. My joy in the process was mitigated by all the delays and frustrations. We much enjoyed being members of the Riga Yacht Club, which was friendly, homely, cosy, and as active in winter as in summer, a popular meeting-place for sailors, ice-yachters and skaters.

The building did not go well. Years later in his book *The Picts and the Martyrs* he wrote "the only boat builder to finish a job on time was Noah, who knew he would be drowned if he didn't." He was becoming increasingly impatient with the progress on the building of the yacht. During March and April he wrote several times to his mother detailing the problems:

To Edith R. Ransome

23 Stralsunder Strasse
Kaiserwald
Riga
March 29 1922

My boat for this year is getting ready for the water. You will be pleased to hear she is twice the size of last year's, a huge creature, thirty feet long and about twelve feet broad so that it will take a miracle to upset her …

Her name is to be Racundra. But it's lucky I bought so much stuff with me from England for her, because it is extremely hard to get anything here …

I suppose some time in May we shall be afloat. Now there is still snow, and the lake is frozen solid and shows no sign of melting. Carts and horses drive across it. Sledges rather.

April 11 1922

My dear Mother,

...Yesterday, however, there was a tug breaking up the ice in the broad arm of the river across which our new boat is lying in a shed...

... I think politics are beastly, and the only thing to do is to forget them for as long periods as possible. This, as soon as we have finished fitting out Racundra, we propose to do...

... So I think that about May 15 I shall be able to set my sails and sail away to the islands of the blest, or rather to the islands of the Damned Thieves who stole my mainsail two years ago. However, this year I shall be living on board all the time, and shall try not to give them a chance...

Your affectionate son,

April 22 1922

The boat in which I shall cruise will not be ready for sea for another month, which is most annoying, as we shall lose about three weeks of good weather ... it is maddening about her not being ready, when we have been howling at the man, and tinkering and hammering has been going on all winter. However, when she is ready, she will be a really stout ship, and it will be our own fault if accidents occur. I have taken the compass down to be fitted in a good place aft of the mizen mast and in front of the steering well. Her appearance when ready will be something like this:

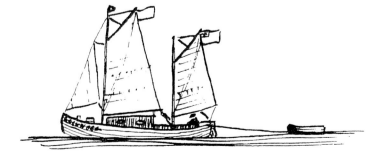

Arthur.

Ransome became increasingly frustrated with the builder and the lack of progress. In June he wrote in detail about the problems to his mother:

June 8 1922
Riga.

My dearest Mother,

We are still wrestling with difficulties here in getting ready for sea. The boat itself is nearly ready, and we are busy with mattresses and things of that kind. But nothing on earth will induce the swine who is alleged to be doing some metal work for the mast to deliver the goods, ordered about three months ago. However, the little tiny motor I am sticking in to push us along in calms is now being installed, though I admit it looks rather toy like, its propeller looking rather like a little brass flower attached to the big hull of the Racundra. You will be pleased to hear that I have persuaded the old man who looks after our dinghy to come with us on the first trip to Reval. He is very ancient (sailed with Lady Brassey in the Sunbeam about the time that I was born) but very efficient, and highly entertaining. He wants to sail to England with me next year. He is quite the best sailor in these parts, and I shall be glad to have him if only to pick up hints from him, to polish up what, hitherto, I have been finding out for myself. I think I can now safely say that on Midsummer Day I shall be able to date a letter to you from on board the Racundra.

During the Whitsun holidays, when the land was a sort of hell of ginger beer bottles, gramophones and waste paper, spread all over the place by family parties, each, of course, accompanied by a dachshund, we spent the whole time on the water in the little boat, and had some very good sailing. I am learning all the time and can now do things in the little boat that I should never have dared in Slug or Kitty, though they were twice the size. It remains to be seen how I shall handle Racundra, but certainly I am much more able to handle her than I was a year ago.

Your Bantam Coffee has been religiously kept (not a tin opened) and lies in a place apart, the first stores to go on board Racundra. Tomorrow I am buying a lifebelt, which I hope will be less useful than the coffee.

But it is very sickening how much of the summer has gone, although perhaps it is as well, for I am not really free to start on a real cruise until the Russian number of the Guardian has gone to press. Still, we could have been living on board, which is a joy in itself, or would have been. Among the joys, which I remember, even one day's sleep in Slug, with stone ballast for pillows, after a thirty-hour sail, stands out. And Racundra will be luxury compared to that. Actually horsehair mattresses.

I wish we could see any chance of making our trip to England this summer. But I think it is impossible. Already too late. Chatterton and other great men tell me that there is such a prevalence of N.W. winds from June on in the North Sea, that it is a miserable job crossing from the east after the end of May. So I suppose I shall have to put that off until next year. However, when at last we get going, I am going to try to keep going as hard as I can, for practice sake, and try to cover in distance the journey to England, even if it will not be in the hoped-for direction. The trip to Reval is about 250 miles. It will be 500 if we go straight there and back. I should very much like to do a thousand miles this year. The trip to England is about 1500 allowing for calling at a number of ports. Well, if I do a thousand this year successfully, what with Reval, Helsingfors, Kunda, Arensburg, Pernau and the other Esthonian ports, I shall be pretty confident of being able to bring Racundra home next year, when you shall motor over to Ramsgate or the Medway or somewhere, and have tea in the cabin under the barometer and clock (which said clock keeps time accurately enough to allow me to navigate with her, and duly find out where I am by observing the sun). My friend Wirgo, the Esthonian Minister in Stockholm, is back in Reval, and wants to come down here to sail up to Reval with me, so we shall probably be four on board and something of a tight squash. However it will make the work easier. He has become as mad on boats as me, and has brought his yacht back from Stockholm, and also a folding boat with which, under sail if you please, he navigates the rivers of Esthonia...

...I may have to visit England during the summer, but can pretty well promise to be home in November for a month. I want to be home then, because there is going to be a big Small Craft Show, at which I am sure to pick up wrinkles, and see a decent little stove and other dodges for Racundra. I am fitting her out just as cheaply as ever I can, with the idea of probably wanting to get really decent things at the Show. It is to be in

"RACUNDRA" IN STINT SEE HARBOUR.

STINT SEE HARBOUR TODAY.

the Agricultural Hall, and will probably be the finest collection of all the latest tweaks ever seen.

This is merely a gabble about nothing.

So I stop.
Your affectionate son,
Arthur.

Ransome's diary records the eventual launching of the boat:

26 June
Boat ready in two months. Two men only working on her.

14 July
Lehnert definitely promises Racundra for Aug. 3.

28th July
Racundra in water.

29th July
Racundra christened.

3 August
Boat not ready.

He wrote to his mother again on August 17th:

To Edith R. Ransome
August 17 1922.
Riga.

My dear Mother,

After all kinds of tribulations which I will not recount in detail, I have got Racundra in the water, taken her away from the swine, and with a couple of workmen have got her almost ready for sea. Ship's papers are ready, and I hope on Saturday to move down to the mouth of the river, starting for Reval (about 250 miles away) with the first S.W. wind. I have slept on board since getting her, the workmen turning up at six and working till dark, and today really all the important things are done. I had to make a new centreboard, the old one being stuck and hopelessly warped, and took her up on the slip, after which I made sail and brought her back to the little harbour all by my wild self. The two workmen hammering away in the cabin did not know we were moving till I had got halfway and they put up astonished heads. She is very easy to manage, and so slow on her helm that I have plenty of time to run about and do things while she takes care of herself. But SLOW. My word. Something terrific. Our motion has a stately leisure-ness about it that is reminiscent of the Middle Ages. I have just come home for clock and barometer, which can now be put up in the cabin. Compass is already there. Lamps polished. Water casks oiled and their hoops painted with silver bronze. Anchors fixed. One on deck. She is riding to the other. Lamp in the cabin fixed. Mattresses now going down. Sweet peas on the cabin table and His Britannic Majesty's Minister coming to tea on board this afternoon.

Everything except final stores, Customs examination, and Insurance is done. By the time you get this, we shall pretty certainly be rolling about somewhere in the middle of Riga Gulf. Please address your next letter c/o British Consulate Reval, Esthonia, marking the envelope "To be called for", as we may be a week or ten days on the way, if we stop for weather or in any port. It will be very jolly to find a letter there when we arrive.

Your affectionate son.
Arthur Ransome

The outstanding work being finished after a fashion, they finally set sail for *Racundra's First Cruise* on August 20th. The cruise took them to the island of Runö (Ruhnu), through the Moon Sound to Reval (Tallinn), across to Helsingfors (Helsinki). They returned via Reval (Tallinn), the Nukke Channel to Hapsal (Haapsalu), then to the island of Dagö (Hiiumaa), Werder (Virtsu) and direct to Riga, arriving on September 26th.

On his return he wrote detailing his plans for a book:

To Edith R. Ransome
October 2 1922
Racundra, Riga.

My dear Mother,

You will by this time have heard of how the equinox flung us home with a flick of his mighty tail after giving us a lively time for a fortnight or so. I wrote at once, but was too tired to tell you much about it, and now the freshness has worn off and you will have to wait for a detailed story till you hear the final chapter of my Log. In the way of writing I did pretty well, and came home with eighty photographs (sixty of which I have still to develop) and over 30,000 words written of my first little sailing book. I want to make it sixty thousand altogether, that's the same length as Bohemia, and I think that when I have revised the stuff I wrote while actually sailing and worked in the material I collected last year, I should have a pretty jolly little book. It fails rather badly however from Mr. Christian's point of view by having no feminine interest whatever. All the dialogue in it is between the Ancient and myself and the various odd folk we met, the most interesting of which were the seal-hunters, armed with eighteenth century flintlocks which might have been used by the Jacobites. Generally it was a pretty successful trip, though with so much bad weather as to make the story seem a little exaggerated to anybody who does not know what a stormy sea the Baltic is, and does not remember that we were cruising during the equinox, which is its worst time. We actually sailed over seven hundred miles.

I am still sleeping on board, for fear of pirates, because of the dark nights and because all my most valued possessions are in the boat, but tomorrow or the next day I hope to get everything ashore. At the beginning of next week she will be hauled out and put in a shed for the winter.

I do not know whether I told you that your much belated Bantam Coffee, meant for last year, provided many comforting drinks in the small hours of the morning. Nothing is more wonderful than the effect of a hot drink on a weary steersman who has been at the tiller all night. I remembered you every time, and drank your health in condensed milk and Bantam many times.

I feel quite confident of being able to sail to England next year. The passage from Reval to Helsingfors is twice as long as that from Dover to Calais, and the worst bit of the journey from one end of the Riga Gulf to the other is as long as from Harwich to Rotterdam, and in many ways far worse, from a sailor's point of view. Racundra managed all this like a bird in the worst possible weather, so if I get free in June next year she ought to make nothing of the trip to England, which should take her about six weeks, going comfortably. But of course, I do not know what next year's work will be, or whether I shall be able to be free for so long. I am very anxious to do it, so as to have a second book ready to follow up Racundra in the Baltic or whatever else we call it. Titles thankfully received.

Of course my greatest joy is the navigation, which went through in all four of the out-of-sight-of-land passages without a hitch. It made all my mugging up of books seem really worth while. The sheer excitement of being out of sight of land for twenty-four hours and then seeing the land appear and finding that you have hit it exactly as you had intended is something not to be equalled in any other way. Incidentally my colour is Indian Red and I am said to be very fat. Fat that is for me.

I shall be working on the book until I start for England, in the hope of having the rough copy pretty complete. Then while in England I want to do the revision and get somebody to help in redrawing charts and things necessary for illustration, so as to be able to leave the book in England finished for publication in the Spring. It's a huge joy really doing a non-political book at last. And in fact it is almost violently non-political, so complete a contrast is it to the things I have had to do during the last few years. I feel almost like a starting author again, and somehow think that this will be a sort of breaking of the ice. Parts of it at any rate I think you'll like, though parts of it may seem too technical. At the same time I do not want to leave them out for I expect the book will be read quite considerably by people like me, and I rejoice in detailed accounts of other people's navigation of difficult bits. The worst trouble is that there are three severe storms in it while at sea, and several which we dodged in harbour, and though the storms were S.E., N.E., S.W. and N.W. and so had each his quite special character, yet even for a sailing book there seems to be a blessed sight too much wind. There are also calms and one beastly fog, besides several days of simply jolly sailing. On the whole it gives a pretty good all round picture of autumn sailing in the Baltic, enough perhaps for the escape from the particular to the general, which is essential for a good book.

I have got so accustomed to writing on board that I may not be able to put a sentence together in a room that does not rock just a little. I wonder whether you will be able to let me have a room to write in at Kemsing while I am in England.

In any case I am enormously looking forward to coming home.
Your affectionate son,

His autobiography takes up the story:

After laying *Racundra* up for the winter very early I went to Russia where I spent about a month. In December I went to England, and in London met my wife and a couple of lawyers to discuss arrangements for our divorce. Then I went to Barmouth where the Collingwoods and Barbara were staying. I took with me the diary-logbook which I kept while we sailed *Racundra*, putting down as fully as possible the happenings of every day. I told the Skald (W.G. Collingwood) that I hoped sometime to make some sort of account of sailing in the Eastern Baltic. He read it and urged me not to wait but to do it at once: "You've got a book there ready-made." I needed no further encouragement, and when I got back to Riga in time for Christmas the book was well advanced.

I finished *Racundra's First Cruise* at Kaiserwald before the end of January 1923 (it was published by Unwin later in the year) and then went to Russia.

Ransome was not completely happy with the book and he wrote to his mother on the 16th January 1923, the day he completed the final draft:

(16th January)
I feel that it betrays the process of learning how to write it, and that only the second half, when I have more or less caught the trick of this kind of anecdotal narrative, is really up to scratch ... I daresay there will be found some few lunatics of my own kind who will like it. And I have learnt a lot from doing it about how to deal with the next.

(20th January)

It has, in parts, a certain pleasantness. In parts, however, I do not much care for it and find it rather dull … Nobody will read it, of course, but I shall he glad to have copies of it to give to one or two folk.

Ransome and Evgenia were by now back in the Baltic. The book was published in July 1923 with a first edition print run of 1500; Ransome's author's copies reached him in Riga on 6th July. There was a picture of the Ancient Mariner on the dust jacket with the words: "No sailing man but will be interested in this account of autumn cruising in the Eastern Baltic. The publishers, whose ignorance of sailing is extensive, found that this misfortune or privilege in no way prevented their enjoyment of the human interest of the book and of a world in which it is not only possible, but easy, to forget that politics exist."

Ransome was obviously pleased with the final result and wrote to his mother on 11th July:

Unwin has made really quite a nice book of it, and I am still full of joy over my new baby, my first non-political book since the war. I fear it will get slanged by my political enemies just the same. But that cannot be helped. Let's hope somebody will find something nice in it. The American publisher writes enthusiastically about it, so I have hopes of the Yanks, though very little at home.

THE WRITING OF RACUNDRA'S FIRST CRUISE

We have already learnt that 30,000 words were already completed on his return from the cruise. He had planned for about 60,000 in the finished book. To achieve this he expanded the purely factual account with additional information and included several chapters of events and experiences from his previous two years sailing in the Baltic. 30 photographs were included, some of which were different from later editions. One of the photographs "Women of Runö coming out of church" was not used again. It shows the stone church that was built next door to the original, and better known, wooden one. There were also four charts included in the book, of which three had to be redrawn to reproduce properly. I believe the fourth, "Helsingfors, showing Nylands Y.C. anchorage", is Ransome's original. He wrote, and added as an appendix, a detailed description of the yacht. The expanded narrative of the cruise brought the length up to approximately 40,000 words. The additional, largely unrelated chapters made up the balance. He was concerned that the book would turn out to be too technical for the general reader. During the letter to his mother on the 2nd October 1922 (see above) he had already expressed his reservations in this respect.

The additional chapters were:

"The Building of *Racundra*" – a brief outline of the many problems encountered and how he came to consider the project.

"The Crew" – Cook (Evgenia), Ancient Mariner (Carl Sehmel), and Master and Owner (Ransome).

"Port of Reval" (Tallinn) – details of history, topography, and life in the capital of Esthonia.

"Baltic Port Old and New" – recollections of his previous visits and the changes he found.

"The Roogö Islands" – description of visits made to the islands the previous year.

"The Ship and the Man" – reprint of the article published in the *Manchester Guardian* on 30th January 1922. The article is an expanded small portion of a substantial unpublished essay titled "On the Pirate Ship". Whilst in Baltic Port (Paldiski North) in late July 1921 he saw a ship, about to embark, that he had previously seen laid up on the island of Roogö (Vaike Pakri). He arranged with the captain to ship as supercargo for the trip. The complete text of this essay is included below.

"Toledo of Leith" – detailed description of a visit made the previous year.

Ransome was happy with the finished book. He visited London in the spring of 1924 to finalise arrangements for his divorce from Ivy, his first wife, and thus leave him free to marry.

Racundra's First Cruise is therefore an account of Arthur and Evgenia's Baltic sailing in the third decade of the last century. In his lifetime he was never to publish another book about *Racundra,* although he fully intended to do so. *Racundra's* second cruise was never turned into a book (he only completed some 6000 words), possibly because the trip was interrupted by work commitments and a weeklong gale in which nothing much happened.

When the Ransomes married in 1924 they took "*Racundra* for a leisurely cruise in the lower reaches of the Dvina, up and down the Aa and up the Bolderaa to that fascinating, mysterious, romantic and claustrophobic maze of shallow narrow channels winding between enormously tall and strong reeds for what feels like thousands of square miles." The full story of this trip is told in *Racundra's Third Cruise*, published by Fernhurst Books in 2002.

Arthur Ransome had at last been able to achieve his aim "to get back to my proper trade of writing" by the publication of his first really successful book, which has become a "Sailing Classic".

ON THE PIRATE SHIP

A week ago, sailing by Roogo, I saw that the pirate ship which at my first coming had been lying nearly high and dry under a little islet between Great and Little Roogo had been hauled off, and was anchored in deep water. Next day I watched her sail under mainsail and staysail across the bay to Baltic Port where she was made fast between anchor and quay, close by the Kittiwake. Men were continually at the pumps, and streams of water poured from her on both sides. Balks of wood had been nailed on her from without and busy carpentry proceeded within, stopping the leaks. I rowed round her in the dinghy and learnt that her name was Venera, but she was a sorely battered Venus. Two great holes had been broken through her planking by the rocks. Her mainmast was rotting; her rigging tattered like a spiders web through which someone has thrust a careless hand. And yet, for all that, she looked more of a pirate ship than ever, a very old ship, but with fine lines at stem and stern, a ship that for all her age and battering would out run the clumsy-bowed potato coasters who lay beside her in the harbour spick and span with new paint and new rigging and freshly tarred hulls. A few days later, I heard that she was to put to sea as soon as she had been patched up, to fetch a cargo of wood from the further end of Dago. Her owner, Hinrikson, was to go with her, and I set off at once to find him and ask if I might travel as supercargo. Could I sail that night? I could sail any minute, of course, flung a few tins of meat from the Kittiwake's stores into a bag, took my bedding, and was ready. However, while waiting at Hinrikson's a man came from the ship to say they could not start, as there were still repairs to do to the bowsprit, the foremast was unrigged, and the leak still considerable. I slept on a sofa at Hinrikson's and next morning at nine o'clock, we took our dunnage to ship. Hinrikson, I should say, is the richest man of Baltic Port, who boasts that he never spends money on anything, dresses like a beggar and is proud of it and employs no one for what he can do himself. A little old man of sixty odd, he packed his things and mine on a handcart and, refusing to hire a man, he and I towed our things down to the harbour and put them on board. The ship had been hauled out of harbour and was moored by the bows to a bollard at the end of the pier. She was in a rare mess. Bits of rope, wire, planks, tools lay about all over her decks. She still leaked. Her masts had not been repaired, and her "pudding jib" was still unready. She looked more like salvaged wreck than a ship about to make a voyage, and the men about the harbour urged me not to sail in her unless I had to. However, she still had the indescribable air of a good ship, the fine lady showing through her rags, and I was more than anxious to see how she would sail. Hinrikson disappeared into the cabin and I turned to with the men to make sail. I will not describe in detail all the things that were found to be unready, the makeshifts, the general happy-go-luckiness of the start. At eleven thirty our hawser was cast loose, and we gathered way under mainsail, mizen, staysail and one jib. There was a fair wind from the north, and we tacked up out of the bay, making sail bit by bit as we went until when we went about for the last time and bore away beyond Roogo we had both topsails up and all three jibs. If she were built too late to be a pirate ship, that old schooner certainly should have been. There were many other vessels sailing west, but we did not sight a single one that we did not overhaul and pass. Said one of sailors, "When the Venera is at sea, all other ships are anchored by the stern" and indeed it seemed so. Even the cutters, which in these seas can usually outsail the schooners seemed to have run aground, or to have been held by a hand from under the sea like the ship in the story of Sadko, and scarcely moved from their places while the Venera overhauled them and left them far behind. There was very little wind, but the water foamed and spurted under her curved bows. By six o'clock we had passed the island of Odensholm, and when dusk came we were already far beyond Worms, and near the point of Takhona, the northern point of Dago. Here the wind fell altogether, and, in a dead calm, even the Venera ceased to make headway.

In the cabin, the skipper, a man of my own age, very quiet, and, so he told me, as new to the Venera as myself, sat down with Hinrikson and myself to make a meal. The skipper had a herring. I had a small tin of bully beef. Hinrikson had a large basket, full of salt herrings, eggs, bread, butter, cold meat and other good things. Hinrikson closed his eyes, said grace, and then set to work on his provisions. He did not offer any to us. This was repeated at each meal, until my provisions were run out (I had given him half my meat and a share in my sardines, and half the apple cakes I had brought from Baltic Port). Then he twice offered me a piece of a large pike, which I had caught myself and given him the previous day. Finally however, when I had nothing left to eat at all, he gave me a piece of bread and also two eggs. But at each meal the skipper and I said no grace and ate dry bread, while Hinrikson enjoyed bread and butter. I do not recall these details in any spirit of complaint, nor will Hinrikson in the least mind the truth. While we were towing our goods on the handcart to the harbour, he, the richest man in the countryside had said to me, "Other people would employ a man. Other people would be ashamed. But I have no shame." It is said of him that he has never given anybody anything in his life, but that his church will be the gainer by his death. He is president of the local Lutheran community and on Sunday goes to sleep in a prominent place amongst the congregation. His carefulness in small matters is part of his character, and I am sure he would not part with it. He is interested in etymology and history. After supper he gave me a lecture on the Plantagenets, informed me that Ivanhoe was the greatest work in English literature, told me that Esthonian and Japanese were kindred languages, and that "Let go" (in dropping the anchor) was not as I supposed an adoption from English but taken from the Swedish "Leggo", from which if we used a similar term we had probably adopted it. As far as present day politics are concerned, he is against all war between Christian nations (this would allow us to punish the Bolsheviks) and regards the Versailles peace as an idiocy, quoting Esthonian proverbs to the point, such as, "Too large a bite spoils the mouth" and saying that we could have had a good peace with good will instead of this peace with mutual hate, added, "Half a good egg is better to eat than a whole one addled".

When it came to sleeping, he told me that he did not like sleeping in the bunks of these old ships, because of the bugs, and drove me from the place I had taken on the floor, took the mattress and went to sleep there himself. I had no mattress, but slept a fine voluminous ample sleep on an old sheepskin coat. If there were bugs, they might have eaten me to the bones and I should not have felt them nor grudged them the meal. I was waked by hearing the order to trim the sails, and tumbled out of the cabin in my breeches in time to bear a hand. A very gentle breeze was now ruffling the water from the northwest, and the Venera, which had hardly moved during the night, began to make headway. Away to leeward was a low coast with trees, the Takhona lighthouse, a little church, and the chimney of a brickfield alone breaking the monotonous line. Far ahead half below the horizon was the cape of Dagorot, below the horizon, so that the higher land looked like a series of wooded islands with shining straits of sea between them.

With an old chart and my pocket compass which I had brought with me from the Kittiwake (for the compass of the Venera was not in working order) we made out where we were, and set a course that should bring up along the coast to a point on the eastern side of Cape Restna. As we came near we saw what seemed to be stacks of wood on the shore, and turned in directly, finding, as we ran in that there was a wooden pier, a discovery that caused great delight as we supposed we should be able to load from the pier instead of from small boats. We anchored some hundreds of yards from this pier, and Hinrikson, the skipper and I rowed ashore in the ship's boat. The coast seemed a solid mass of pinewoods, and our hopes fell as we found that the pier had been partly destroyed, but rose when among the pines. Close to the

shore we saw a fair sized sailing ship nearly finished, the raw wood of her
gleaming in the threads of sunlight that fell upon her through the trees. At
least there must be people here, since a ship was being built. But we could
see no one about her, and, but for the ruined pier, and that golden hull in the
shadows under the tall pines, the coast might have been that of an
uninhabited island. There was not a sign of human life, and no land noises
except the calls of a woodpecker somewhere in the forest that ran right down
almost to the water's edge. We rowed in between sunken rocks and grounded
our boat on a shore of small pebbles, and after pulling her up, made for the
ship among the trees. There was a rough railing round her, and we went
through looking at the hull, and admiring the workmanship thereof, which
was indeed very fine. A little behind her, quite invisible from a few yards
away in the thick wood, we came on a tiny clearing, with a loud noise of
grasshoppers, a hayfield not much bigger than a small suburban garden, a
cornfield perhaps three times the size, and a log hut with deep thatched roof.
Still there was no sign of life. No dog barked, and no one answered when we
knocked at the door. We lifted the wooden latch and walked in. The hut was
divided in two parts. In one were a couple of spinning wheels, one very old,
black with age, and another, seemingly new, a precise copy of the first. There
was a wooden bed, and a great chest, and a wooden stool or two, all made as
if to last forever. A very little light came through the small windows. The
second room held nothing except a stove and a big hand loom for weaving,
with some grand strong cloth being made upon it, meant, I think, for the sails
of the still unfinished ship. A few clean cooking things were hanging over the
stove, and fishing lines and nets were hanging on the walls. We walked out,
and, leaning on the gate into the cornfield, as if he had been there all the
time, an old man stood watching us. He had steel grey curly hair, and eyes
of very dark blue. The skin of his face was clear walnut. He reminded me a
little of the fine old head of Edward Carpenter. His clothes were all of some
strong homespun cloth, probably made on the loom we had seen, and on his
bare feet were shoes made, I think, of woven string with soles of thick rope.
With his arrival the whole place seemed to have sprung to life. He was
accompanied by three sheep, and two pigs snuffled in the ground close by.
Hens also came clucking round his feet, and a dog, as impassive as his
master, lay beside the gate, half opening his eyes as if he had been awaked
from sleep. He told us that our wood was not there, and told us further where
to land further eastward on the coast to find the cottage of the forester which
was some way from the shore. I tried to buy eggs and butter from him, but
he said that he had no eggs and never made more butter than he needed. We
should get some from the forester, perhaps. Whether he had wife and child,
I do not know. I saw no signs of them, nor of any men who could be helping
him in the building of that ship which was so very much larger than his own

hut. The bit of coast where he lived is called Ermuste, that is, "The Terrible", for its rocks and the roughness of the sea there. It is a place of many wrecks. I wondered how many this aged Robinson Crusoe had watched with those dark blue eyes of his, impassively as he watched us now, indifferent as fate or as the sea itself.

We hurried back to the shore, Hinrikson being anxious to find his wood and set about loading it while the sea was comparatively smooth. Before we reached the ship, the skipper stood in the boat and yelled to the men to be getting the anchor up, and in a minute or two we had our staysail and jibs up, and were sailing eastwards again along the coast to Polli. Here again there were signs of houses to be seen from the ship, but a large schooner was anchored off the shore, and boats laden with timber till the water lapped the gunwale were being paddled off to her and then thrown chunk-by-chunk, overhand up on deck where they were caught and stowed by those aboard her. Considerable stacks of wood were arranged on the beach above high-water mark. Again we landed and after a couple of miles walk through the forest came to the forester's cottage and, finding no one, ate wild strawberries which grew in great profusion, slept for a little, and were wakened by his wife who with much polite ceremonial of repeated handshaking directed us to follow a path through the trees till we should find him. We walked on and found the forester and his son stowing the last of their hay into a thatched hayshed in a clearing. The forester came down from the top of the hay where he was stamping into place the forkfuls tossed up by his son, and we all sat on the ground and lit pipes while he and Hinrikson discussed the question of our wood, which it appeared was not where we expected to find it, but beyond Ermuste, close under the point of Restna. We went back to the shore and while Hinrikson bargained with the men and girls who were loading the wood for the schooner lying off, I watched them at their work. The timber, sawn into short balks, was loaded on little rough carts which, pulled by horses were drawn out into the sea. Girls walked into the sea with them, and stood nearly waist deep in water while they transferred the wood to the little boats, which came alongside the carts. Then men and boys sitting on the bows of the boats invisible from the stern behind the pile of wood, rowed off to the ship and tied alongside flung the wood up and over so quickly that it was as if a continual fountain of wood spurted over the ship from each boat.

While we had been in the forest the wind had risen and veered a little eastwards. Waves were breaking on the beach, and our boat had been swung round and was half full of water, getting finally swamped just as we got her off. However we got going and baled as we went. We rowed to the strange schooner, as our skipper had not been here before and wished to consult about anchorages. We were told it was unsafe to stay here for the night but that there was a sheltered anchorage at Luidja still further eastwards, in a bay on the western side of Takhona. After long-tacking we made this bay and ran in anchoring close to another vessel, which with the tack of her mainsail clewed up looked against the sunset like a big seabird with her head under her wing for the night.

In the morning of Friday the wind had freshened from the east, and we ran before it, passed Polli and Ermuste to the place where our wood actually was, but standing in near the shore we found such waves breaking on the beach that it would have been impossible to go ashore, still less to land wood, and had shoal water visible close ahead of us, so that the skipper, a quiet fellow with a face usually without expression of any kind, showed visible and audible relief when we gave up the idea of landing, and bore up for open sea, only just in time, it seemed, as we could see the rocks which we should certainly not have been able to avoid had we held another minute on our course. There is no sea like the Baltic for shortness of temper. After a fine morning the wind rose and the waves with it, and we had to furl our topsails, and take in two jibs, and even so, had a heavy time of it. The Venera, unloaded, was blown to leeward like a basket, and, having found that she was a little uncertain in going about under such conditions, and not one of us knowing the coast, we stood right out to sea, to make Luidja in a single tack. We sailed closehauled till out of sight of land, and then, after one false start, awkward enough in such a wind, went about, one of the sailors and I holding the boomed staysail aback by brute force. After an hour or two, the skipper, very pleased and proud came into the cabin with the news that he had judged just right and that we could afford to bear away a little, since the masts of the ship we left at anchor at Luidja Bay were to be seen on the horizon over the starboard bow. Early in the afternoon we dropped anchor in fairly smooth water, though, with the wind blowing overhead we lowered all our sails, as had the other ship.

There was then a serious consultation. With the wind as it was it would be impossible to load the wood. If the wind fell during the night it would only be possible to load on Saturday morning, even if it were possible to get the labourers together and they were at Ristna to meet us when we arrived. On Saturday afternoon the labourers would not work except for extra pay and Hinrikson would never give extra pay for anything, nor would he, on principle, regardless of the weather, allow work on Sunday. That meant that instead of returning by Sunday as we had hoped, the Venera would be here for another five days at least, perhaps longer. I decided to see more of Dago, by landing at Luidja, and making my way overland across the island. On the horizon I could see the spire of a church. Well, a church meant a pastor, and a pastor meant lodging for the night. I committed to memory the Esthonian for "Please may I sleep on your hay" "lubage mind henute piale magama", in all these parts the hayloft being the best spare room for visitors, and indeed, as I found when I stayed with the fishermen at Harko, used sometimes as a sleeping place for the whole family. At the point of the bay furthest from the church there were stacks of wood lying, and Hinrikson wanted to look at them and perhaps find somewhere near them someone who could tell him more about the wood he was looking for. So he took the boat and a sailor and I flung my sleeping bag into my knapsack and went with them.

The shore where we landed was flat and deep in ooze, which came to our knees as we waded out pulling the boat with us. Close behind the woodpiles we found a good road, and beyond it a cottage and outhouses and a very pretty girl feeding hens. She saw us coming, and, like a good Esthonian, instantly pretended she had not and walked slowly off, at first taking no notice even of our shouts. At last however, when Hinrikson shouted a definite question in Esthonian she turned round. Hinrikson solemnly introduced himself, the sailor and me, and there was a great ceremony of handshaking. The pretty girl told him that her father was the wood-keeper, and would be back later in the evening, and then, on learning that I wanted to go to Heltermaa, she said that the very road that ran past the door would take me alike to Kardla and to Heltermaa, and that if only I had come half an hour earlier, people had driven by going to Kardla, who could have taken me with them. She proposed that I should wait in the cottage until others should drive by, but said there might be none as it was already six in the evening. She spoke a little Russian. I decided however to be getting on my way at once, and, after a double round of handshaking, and a farewell glance through the trees to that old pirate ship, looking more rakish and piratish than ever as she lay at anchor beside the other ship with the usual blunt bows of the Dago coasters, I got my knapsack, which was inexorably heavy, on my back and set off to make my way to the other end of Dago. The road lay through little woods, small birches, mountain ash, beeches, unfenced, the grass beneath them cut for hay and running to the side of the road. Then it opened out on wide sand flats, grass covered on which cattle and horses were grazing. The road cut away from the sea in a wide peninsula, but here and there on the landward side of it were wide shallow lakes, of salt water, which, when the wind raises the water on this side of the Baltic, are joined to the sea. I passed through a small village, but saw no living creature except a dog and two bulls who were trotting steadily through the village, on the way, I expect, from one sand flat to another where they thought the grass was better. I met however several people on the road in their little springless carts, a gay rug covering the hay, and here and there among the cattle were cowherds, small boys, or little girls, and an old woman knitting as she watched her beasts. I had thought of sleeping out, but in the only shop I passed I could not get either milk or eggs and I had only the last relic of a dry crust. So I pushed on, and late in the evening came to the parish church of Reigi.

Now Reigi is close by the cape of Korgesaar, and is one of those innocent places which are making up by long years of blameless life for the wickedness committed in their lurid past. However many worthy farmers sleep in the pews on Sundays, however many prayers are said, nothing can undo the old evil that was done in this place when Baron Ungern Sternberg lived, just over there, under the woods on the cape, within sight of this place, and made a treacherous dangerous coast still more treacherous and dangerous by ingeniously setting lights among the rocks in such places that they would set sailors out of their reckoning, and bring ships on the rocks when Ungern Sternberg and his merry men, no doubt the ancestors of the present population, profited by the cargoes, and made short work of survivors lest these, spreading their wrongs abroad, should put an end to a means of livelihood almost as interesting as fishing, and with something of the same art of lure and profit by the trustfulness of others. Yet it is possible that they could have spared survivors freely, for tradition dies hard, and along the rocky Esthonian coast, from ancient times the people have counted wrecks as gifts from God and their own inalienable property. In 1287, the Governor of Reval refused to compensate Lubeck for a wreck on the Esthonian coast, and the cargo, which had been seized by Esthonians, alleging that it was "Strandgut", and that it was the property of the finders. Ungern Sternberg lived just over a hundred years ago, and, at the present day, the islanders of Tutters look to make part of their living by wrecks, and those of Worms, only two years ago, pulled even the engines of a stranded British ship to pieces for the sake of the copper in it, which they wanted to make rivets for their boats, and the iron nuts, which are so much more convenient than stones as sinkers for fishing nets.

The church, tall for its length, white, with a grey spire, stands among trees. It is a Lutheran church, and the Germans had a curious habit of building gin houses precisely opposite the church door (many such are to be seen in Esthonia), in old days making it possible to tie up one's horse at the gin shop, go to church, and get drunk afterwards to lessen the tedium of the drive home. Many churches, where there is no gin shop, have a row of stout posts outside the church wall, with long timbers fastened on the top of them, for the tying up of horses. I have often seen ten, twenty, thirty little carts, each with the gaudy rugs that are the pride of the country, fastened up outside the churches on a Sunday, and the long timbers were nearly always falling to pieces with the steady gnawing of the horses. What the timbers were to the horse, I suppose the gin shop was meant to be to the parishioners. Here at Reigi, sure enough, exactly opposite the gate under the trees leading to the church was the characteristic low white building, and I went in at once, knowing that there at least I might be able to get something to eat.

But the gin shop was a gin shop no longer. On the one time bar were newspapers. On the bottle shelves were books, and sitting on the deep window ledge were two young women, one of whom could talk Russian. She told me that neither milk, nor eggs nor beer nor anything else was sold there any longer, but that I could read the latest newspapers. I disguised my disappointment and my disgust on meeting newspapers, from which, throughout the summer, I had been most successful in avoiding, and asked where the pastor lived. I was told to turn behind the one time gin shop, when I would find a path leading directly to the pastor's house. I then perceived another object in this strange continual juxtaposition of church and drinking shop. The straight path, from his house to the church and back again, led the pastor within three yards of the gin shop door. For a dour man, what ready material for sermons, for a humane, what constant reminder of the world in which his listeners lived. I saw hollow cheeked thin mouthed pastors turning the other way as they passed, to thunder from the pulpit on the proximity of hell's mouth, and fat jolly ones, nodding to their flock as they went by, and luring the innkeeper, from bar to pew by their own good nature, and perhaps joining their parishioners in a friendly draught after preaching and listening to a dry sermon on a summer's day. But the potato spirit of the country, which makes some cheerful and others pull out their knives, the vodka, with which, in old days, Esthonia supplied a considerable part of Russia, is not a thing for friendly draughts. A hot and bitter spirit, tossed hastily to the back of the throat, it has few virtues and a beastly taste.

You should understand that there was no village by this church. Indeed, in this country of farmers, there seldom is. The church is set in a convenient place, somewhere in the middle of a vast parish, and the congregation drive to it from five, six, ten and even twenty miles round. A mile or so away, beyond an inlet of the sea, were houses among trees, one of them built on the site of Ungern Sternberg's wrecker's stronghold, and still containing his furniture. Far away over the fields were small wooden farms. But church, ex-gin shop, and the pastor's house were alone.

"RACUNDRA" AT REVAL, ESTHONIA.

"RACUNDRA'S" FIRST CRUISE

BY
ARTHUR RANSOME

TO
"RACUNDRA'S" ESTHONIAN FRIENDS

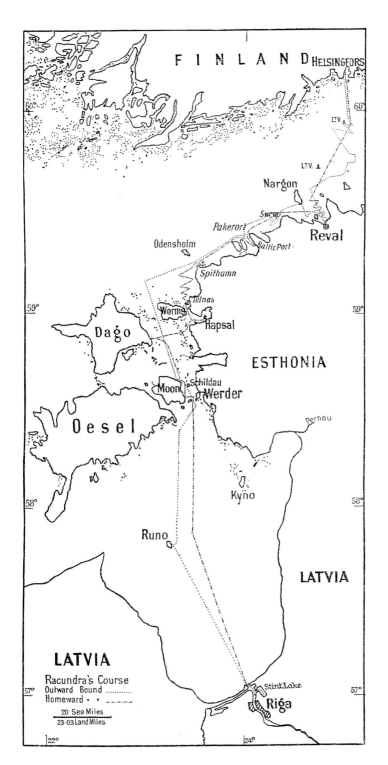

CHART OF THE FIRST CRUISE.

AUTHOR'S NOTE

More than once in the log of *Racundra's* little voyage I have mentioned that I found changes made by the war unrecorded in the obtainable charts. I have just received from the Esthonian Admiralty, through Mr. Edward Wirgo, a set of charts they have recently issued which cover the whole of the delightful cruising ground among the islands, and should certainly be obtained by the skippers of any other little ships who think of visiting these waters.

CONTENTS

ORIGINAL ILLUSTRATIONS

CHARTS

PHOTOGRAPHS

"RACUNDRA'S" FIRST CRUISE

THE BUILDING OF "RACUNDRA"

Houses are but badly built boats so firmly aground that you cannot think of moving them. They are definitely inferior things, belonging to the vegetable not the animal world, rooted and stationary, incapable of gay transition. I admit, doubtfully, as exceptions, snail-shells and caravans. The desire to build a house is the tired wish of a man content thenceforward with a single anchorage. The desire to build a boat is the desire of youth, unwilling yet to accept the idea of a final resting-place.

It is for that reason, perhaps, that, when it comes, the desire to build a boat is one of those that cannot be resisted. It begins as a little cloud on a serene horizon. It ends by covering the whole sky, so that you can think of nothing else. You must build to regain your freedom. And always you comfort yourself with the thought that yours will be the perfect boat, the boat that you may search the harbours of the world for and not find.

That is the story of *Racundra*. Years of planning went into her before ever a line was drawn on paper. She was to be a cruising boat that one man could manage if need be, but on which three could live comfortably. She was to have writing-table and bookcase, a place for a typewriter, broad bunks where a man might lay him down and rest without bruising knee and elbow with each unconsidered movement. She was

"RACUNDRA" ON THE STOCKS.

"RACUNDRA" LAUNCHED.

to carry her dinghy on deck to avoid that troublesome business of towing, which has brought so many good dinghies to their latter end. She should not be fast, but she should be fit to keep the sea when other little boats were scuttling for shelter. In fact, she was to be the boat that every man would wish who likes to move from port to port – a little ship in which, in temperate climates, a man might live from year's end to year's end.

Then came friendship with a designer, the best designer in the Baltic, whose racing boats carried away prize after prize in the old days before the war, whose little cruisers put to sea when steamers stayed in port. And after that *Racundra* began to exist on paper. There were the lines of that stout nose of hers, of that stern, like the sterns of the Norwegian pilot cutters. On paper, I could sit at the writing-table a full yard square, in the cabin where (the measurements proved it) I could stand up and walk about with unbruised head. On paper was that little cockpit where one man, sitting alone, could control the little ship as she made her steady way over the waters. Then came the sail-plan, after how many alterations; a snug rig; you could reach the end of the mizen boom from the deck and there was no bowsprit. The size of the mizen was such that you could keep the sea and keep up to the wind with mizen and foresail alone. The balance of the sails was such (again on paper) that if you wished you could sail under mainsail only, or under main and mizen, so that you could take down your staysail before coming into port and so have a clear deck for playing with warps and anchor chain. *Racundra*, on paper, grew in virtue daily.

It had come to such a pass that I woke from dreams at night sitting in that paper cockpit, with a paper tiller under my arm, steering a paper ship across uncharted seas. *Racundra* had to be built. There was no escape. But my friend the designer, Otto Eggers, lived in Reval, and since the war had had no yard, or he would have built her himself, since the two years of paper boat-building had made him share my madness. But there was no help for it. He could not build. I had to build somewhere else, and, since I was to be in Riga, came to terms with a Riga builder.

I pass over as briefly as I may the wretched story of the building and the hundred journeys over the ice to the little shed in which *Racundra* slowly turned from dream into reality. She was to have been finished in April. She was promised to me on May 1st, May 15th, May 20th and at short intervals thenceforward. She was launched, a mere hull, on July 28th. I went for the hundred and first time to the yard and found *Racundra* in the water. The Lettish workmen by trickery got the builder and me close together, planted us suddenly on a wooden bench which they had decked with beanflowers stolen from a neighbouring garden and lifted us, full of mutual hatred, shoulder high. The ship was launched. Yes, but the summer was over, and there had been whole weeks when *Racundra* had not progressed at all while the builder and his men did other work He promised then that she should be ready to put to sea on August 3rd. She was not. On August 5th I went to the yard and took away the boat unfinished. Not a sail was setting properly. There were no cleats fixed. The centreboard was half up, half down and firmly stuck. But, under power and sails, somehow or other, I got the ship away and took her round to the lake, had her out on the Yacht Club slip, removed the centreboard, had a new one built, re-launched her, and just over a fortnight later turned the carpenters out of her and put to sea.

But there is no use in reminding myself now of those miserable angry months of waiting, in remembering the lacquer that was not put on, the ungalvanized nails that I had laboriously to remove from the cabin work and replace with brass screws. The hull of *Racundra* was right enough, and, by the time we had finished with her, we had put right the lesser matters that were wrong. Fools build and wise men buy. Well, I shall never build again, and in all probability shall never have money enough to buy. Nor shall I have need. For *Racundra* turned out to be all that I had hoped. We took her to sea in the Baltic autumn; we had her at sea when big steamers reported damage from the heavy weather, and never for a minute did she show the smallest sign of disquiet.

Weather that was good enough for us was good enough for her, and, when the Equinox flung her home with a last flick of his mighty tail, she sailed through the rollers on the bar and up the troubled Dvina, demure, serene, neat, as if she were returning from a day's trip in June.

For those who are interested in such things, there is a detailed description of *Racundra* at the end of this book. Here it is enough to say that she is a centreboard ketch just under thirty feet long with a small auxiliary motor. It is a five-horsepower motor, but, possibly on account of my inexperience, it seemed to need forty horsepower to start it, for which reason I did not use it at all during the voyage.

THE CREW

AND now for the crew. There were three of us. There was the Cook, to whom, I think, is due most of the credit for the ease and pleasantness of our voyage. She can take her trick at the tiller if need be, but that, for her, is holiday. All the hard work was hers. She cooked a meal. It was eaten. She washed up and, just as the dry dishes reached the rack, one or other of that hungry company would inquire whether or no the time for the next meal was drawing near. She cooked another meal. As its last remains were cleared away, as sure as fate she would catch the eye of one or other of us looking hungrily at the clock. We, of course, navigating, sailing, had our strenuous moments, after which would follow long hours of plain and easy steering. She, on the other hand, thanks to our appetites, became a sort of juggler, keeping plates, cups, saucepans, kettles, teapot, coffee-pot, thermos flasks and Primuses in a whirl of perpetual motion. We, in harbour, idled, fished, and watched the barometer and the weather, sustaining our self-respect by oracular utterance. She, in harbour as at sea, never for a moment was able to give those pots and pans a rest. She might have been dancing on swords and juggling with knives where an instant's pause meant death. We saw her throughout the day in a cloud of cooking, and the steersman at night, looking down the companion, saw always busy hands cleaning obstinate aluminium, and he who rested on his bunk heard, as he turned in comfortable sleep, the chink of crockery and the splash of washing up. The Primuses roared continually, like the blast furnaces in northern England. And we, relentless and without shame, called continually for food. Of the three of us, the Cook, without a doubt, was the one who worked her passage.

The second of us was the Ancient Mariner. On the Stint See at Riga was a tiny harbour for small boats, where during the long months of waiting for *Racundra* I had kept my dinghy. There, in a little wooden hut on a raft, lived an old seaman, the harbourmaster of this Lilliput port. On my first coming he had spoken a few words of English. Gradually, day by day, the language came back to him, and with the language memories of a life he had almost forgotten. Many, many years ago he had sailed from Southampton in the famous *Sunbeam* of Lord Brassey. He had spent fifteen years of his youth in Australia. He had shared in the glorious runs of the old tea clippers. He had been a seaman in the *Thermopylae*, which he called the *Demooply*, and had raced in her against the *Kutuzak*, in which odd Russianized name I recognized the *Cutty Sark*. And now he was taking care of ten-foot dinghies, and every morning made a voyage across the lake in a rowing-boat with a leg-of-mutton sail to bring the milk from a farm on the other side. He took care of my sailing dinghy as if she had been an ocean liner, made her a padded wharf to preserve her varnish, and spoke of her quick passages across the little lake as if she were a clipper returning round the Horn. He and I became friends, and long before *Racundra* was finished, knowing that I had planned a voyage to England, he went to see her in her shed and, returning, begged me to take him with me. "I am an old man," he said, "and I should like once more to go to sea before it is too late." And I, of course, agreed with joy, for there is no such rigger in the Baltic as the Ancient Mariner who has known what it was to sail in the *Thermopylae* in the days of her pride.

Then, as the months passed, and we knew that the builder had made the English voyage impossible this year, it was decided that he should come with *Racundra* on her first cruise. He spoke of *Racundra* always as "our ship", and, as we sailed, his ambitions for her grew with every day. "When we are in the Mediterranean," he would say, "we must make a canvas double roof for the cabin or it will be too hot in there."

And then, "She'll find the long waves of the Atlantic child's play after this. It won't be till she is near the American coast that she'll have anything as bad." He, that Ancient Mariner, was on this miniature cruise as happy as a boy. Nothing would make him leave the ship. He never went ashore, except in Helsingfors to look for a particular size of sailmaker's needles, unobtainable in Riga, and in smaller ports to bring water to refill our casks. "Shore," he would say, "I have enough of shore at home." He was a very little man, with a white beard and a head as bald as my own. Sometimes on board he wore a crimson stocking-cap with a tassel, when he looked like a gnome, a pixy or a fairy cobbler. If Queen Mab went to sea she could not find a fitter mariner.

The third of us was *Racundra's* "master and owner", who writes these words even now with the swelling pride that he felt when he first saw them on the ship's papers handed to him on departure by the Lettish Customs Office. "Master and Owner of the *Racundra*." Does any man need a prouder title or description? In moments of humiliation, those are the words that I shall whisper to myself for comfort. I ask no others on my grave.

THE START

ON August 19th I got rid of the carpenters, near ten o'clock in the evening, and spent the better part of the night in clearing overboard the mess they had left behind them. A good deal of the mess they had, after the manner of carpenters, built into the boat, and I shall not be able to get rid of it until during the winter I undo much of the work they did. Much of the work they were supposed to do they had not done, but I had suffered enough from them, and learnt that they were prepared to work for another two years on the boat if I should allow them. If only to save her from them I had to put to sea. The inside of the boat was unpainted, except that I had slapped a single coat over the cabin walls and cupboards, doing one side first and, when that was dry, shifting all the litter across the cabin and painting the other side. An incredible amount remained to be done. But it was already very late for cruising in these parts, and the last of the yachts that had left Riga for summer voyages had returned for the winter before ever we left that little harbour in the lake. So, though locks did not work, though there were no fastenings to the forehatch and none to the companion-way, though forecastle and kitchen were still raw unpainted wood, though cleats were lying about not yet fastened into the decks, though we had only half a dozen blocks worthy of the name, the rest being the clumsiest makeshifts, we knew that if we did not start at once we should not start till next year. We three looked her all over and decided to get away anyhow and finish things up on the voyage.

I slept in *Racundra* that night, as I had done for the last two weeks, but for the first time slept in a cabin not half full of shavings and carpenters' tools. At 5.30 in the morning

THE ANCIENT MARINER AT THE TILLER.

FIRST SIGHT OF LAND (RUNÖ ISLAND).

of August 20th I jumped overboard for the last time in the Stint See and swam round *Racundra* as usual while porridge was cooking on the Primus. An hour later the Ancient Mariner came on board, followed presently by the Cook. The wind was N.W., and we were able to slip with it out of the little harbour and reach the whole way down the lake to the entrance to the Mühlgraben, which connects the lake with the Dvina River. There was not much wind, and we had time to screw in the cleats for the staysail sheets before we had any tacking to do. All three sails were setting abominably, as we had no battens for them, the builder having failed us. I had decided to make the trip to Reval without them, knowing that I could there get them properly made.

The entrance to the Mühlgraben is narrow, and in tacking through it, *Racundra* refused to stay and ran her centreboard into the mud. We got off, however, by pulling the board up a few inches, after which there were no more shallows, and we crawled very slowly from side to side between the canal wharves and the balks on the other side which cage a sea of floating timbers. A British steamship, the *Baltabor*, was loading in the Mühlgraben, and Captain Whalley, who has known *Racundra* from her birth, since he visited her in the builder's shed, was on the bridge as we struggled by. The Ancient and I had agreed that two leads were unnecessary, and had therefore each left his own lead at home, so I hailed Whalley as we passed and begged the loan of a five-pounder. *Racundra* went on, zigzagging obstinately through the narrow canal, while I tumbled into the dinghy and dropped back and hung on to *Baltabor's* ladder while the lead was found and lowered away to me. We should often have been in a sore pickle without it.

I thought we should probably be all day getting through the Customs at the far end of Mühlgraben, and therefore asked Captain Whalley to luncheon on the *Racundra*; and he, who accepted, must afterwards have had the blackest thoughts of me, for, as it turned out, we were held up for only half an hour, and decided to work on to the Winter Harbour at the mouth of the Dvina, hoping to make our peace with Whalley when we should meet him in Reval, where the *Baltabor* was to call.

The Customs House at Mühlgraben is a little yellow wooden building, with flowers in the window and a wicket-gate in a wooden paling on the quay. It stands at the corner where the Red Dvina joins the Mühlgraben, and we let go anchor off it, on the windward side of the channel. I hurriedly discarded my disreputables and put on creased trousers and newly pipe-clayed shoes, in order to make up as far as I could for the "un-yachty" appearance of *Racundra*, a trait of hers which is normally our joy, but is likely to increase the difficulty of dealing with officials. *Racundra* lay there, a regular little ship, "a proper contrabandist", as she has been described, looking, with her ochre topsides and sharp stern, exactly like any one of a hundred Baltic smugglers, while her "owner and master" paddled himself ashore in the very neatest of new varnished dinghies, looking as idly rich as he was in reality busy and poor. It was ten o'clock precisely, and as I had given this time in arranging yesterday with the Chief Customs Office in Riga, I felt our punctuality as a sort of moral pipe-clay and, papers in hand, tapped at the door of the little yellow house with a most satisfactory confidence. I found there a charming young man who talked English and gave me a certificate of clearance without any fuss. He rang up the dock police on the telephone. A harbour policeman, together with a Customs officer from the town, had arrived as the clock was striking, and, everybody being delighted by his own and everybody else's punctuality (the rarest of all things in Eastern Europe), and this being the first occasion on which a foreign-going yacht had been cleared here, passports were stamped in two minutes, another certificate added to the first, after which all three officials left the little wooden house with me, to visit *Racundra* and, by drinking vodka on board, to fulfil the last formalities.

When they saw my dinghy swinging like a nutshell below the lofty wooden landing-stage, they refused emphatically to travel in her, wrongly thinking that she could carry only one. They took a boat of their own, and I rowed off as hard as I could and got a bottle of vodka open and mugs on the cabin table before they arrived. We gave them bread and butter, ham and vodka, and they gave us good wishes and the completest freedom from the red tape in which, had they chosen, they could have tangled us as spiders tangle flies. Twenty minutes after our first arrival, they were pushing off again and we were free, our papers stamped, *Racundra* cleared for foreign parts and already, as it were, abroad.

Elated by this, we gave only half a thought to Whalley. There was still so much to do on board. More cleats to be fixed, backstays rigged, brass bollards substituted for the sharp edged rubbish with which she had been disfigured, and we were all for pressing on down to the river mouth, to the Winter Harbour, where we could lie in peace, finish our work and be ready to slip out into the Gulf the moment the wind should favour us.

We beat out into the broad Dvina River. There was very little current to help us, though I remember early in the spring the current was so strong that sailing upstream in the *Frida*, a little trading cutter, against a local smack, the race was decided by the fact that the other boat passed us stern first, going backwards, while we were just able to hold our ground, and that in a good wind with the water foaming under the bows of both boats. On this occasion we were not so fortunate, and while we were wearily beating down the river we were passed with the utmost ease by a little racing sloop from Riga, sailed by a friend of ours, "the cavalry sailor", a young man who had often amused us during the summer by his habit of coming aboard straight from his barracks and wearing high boots and spurs when on his boat. He went by at what seemed to be a great speed, and turned into the Bolderaa, a tributary of the Dvina, after hailing us and wishing us luck. "He wouldn't pass us like that if we were at sea in anything of a wind," said the Ancient, and we were glad to be comforted, for it is not pleasant to be passed even by a racing boat.

There was plenty of shipping in the Dvina and several coasters were lying at anchor near the mouth of the river, evidently thinking that the northerly wind was not done with us yet. The sight of them confirmed us in our intention of stopping in the Winter Harbour for long enough to get things shipshape, and at ten minutes to two *Racundra*, after raising our spirits by showing what she could do with the wind behind her, when we put the helm up to run back into the harbour, was swinging to her anchor in a good berth near the red railway bridge.

There were clouds in the N.W. after luncheon, but we had a few hours of warm sunshine, and, while we worked on the boat, the Cook went ashore. She said that after seeing what we could do with in the way of luncheon she was afraid she had not enough provisions. We told her that there was a time-honoured rule of the sea: "If grub runs out, eat the Cook." She went ashore in the dinghy with little hope, as it was Sunday, but came back with eggs, black currants, radishes, an extra hunk of cheese and some more potatoes, to find *Racundra* really looking more like herself, with backstays rigged, boards for the sidelights fixed to the shrouds, the compass screwed in its place, gimbals set for the Primus stove, and the cabin-lamp rescrewed on the case of the centreboard chain (which runs up through the cabin roof) in a position where it could no longer split the ceiling by excessive fervour.

But while she had been away the weather had grown worse. Dark enamel clouds in long banks were drifting up; the wind, still against us, was increasing, and rain was visibly on its way towards us. A Dane and a German had joined the anchored coasters in the river, and we were ready to accept their judgment and spend one more night before putting to sea. The Cook started the Primus. The Ancient and I went on with our work on deck, but, nervous for my new sails I broke off to put the covers on the main and mizen, unshackled the staysail sheets, and stuffed the rolled up staysail into a canvas kit-bag. I had just finished as the first drops fell. The wind suddenly grew really strong. *Racundra* snubbed at her chain once: only once, for we were letting out more chain before she could do it again. And then came rain, rainbows, lightning, thunder and squalls all together, and we were glad to close the companion hatch behind us and settle down to a meal in the cabin, and then to smoke and look at charts and be glad we had not started. It grew dark, and through the cabin windows we could see the lights of the coasters and the foreigners heaving violently in the swell that came in from the river mouth.

The dinghy lay astern, fast by her painter to one of the newly fixed cleats. "Would she be stolen?" I asked, remembering the loss of a mainsail in Lahepe Bay and the many tales the Ancient had told me of such lamentable happenings. "It is better here than in the Mühlgraben," said he. "Now, if we had stayed there we should 'a had to put a watch on her all night." He went on to tell a story of a German captain who put his head out of the deck-house in answer to a call out of the dark, and found a man in a boat alongside, holding up the end of a rope. " 'Good rope, sir,' says the man, 'and going cheap. I don't rightly know myself how much there is of it, but for so much, I'll sell you the coil.' The captain looks at the rope and sees that it was right enough. He takes that rope on board, the man in the boat passing it in to him hand-over-hand. There was a big coil, and he paid for it and turned in. In the morning he calls the mate and tells him what a bargain he had made in the night. 'As good rope,' says he, 'as ever I brought with me from Hamburg. Why,' says he, with one foot on the cabin floor and the sleep dropping from his eyes, 'it might be the same rope and for a quarter the price.' And indeed it was the same rope, for them thieves in the Mühlgraben, they had just taken the end of the rope off the foredeck and brought it along aft outside and sold it in on board again, and everybody in the Mühlgraben was telling that story afterwards, everybody but one man, and that was the Dutchy captain who had made such a wonderful bargain."

WOMEN OF RUNÖ COMING OUT OF CHURCH.

WOMEN AT RUNÖ CHURCH TODAY.

RIGA TO RUNÖ

BY nine in the morning of the 21st, the wind had shifted to the west. There was sunshine and, in the river, the coasting schooners were getting under way. So we hoisted sails, learnt that our windlass was useless, got our anchor by hand, and made off out of the harbour for the mouth of the river. A heavy swell was coming in; there was still plenty of wind, and we were much annoyed to be held up by a hail from a man on the Customs House Quay at Dünamünde. We had thought that yesterday's ceremony at Mühlgraben had left us definitely cleared, but it seemed that we had to hand over here the certificate I had got from the Riga Customs. The swell was so big that I was more than half afraid of smashing *Racundra* against the pier. The man explained by shouts what he wanted, and we sailed as near as I thought we safely could, wrapped the certificate in a rag, with a bit of chain as a makeweight, and threw it on the pier as we cavorted past. The man grabbed it, opened it, and waved his hand down the river. We were free.

Racundra switchbacked over the swell, taking only a drop or two of water over her nose as she dipped and then lifting easily enough, but taking fountains of water through her centreboard case, the top of which had been left uncaulked. That, however, we put right in a minute or two. And then, just as we cleared the moles, the wind suddenly fell away almost to nothing, while the swell remained and we rolled about so uncomfortably that only iron-fastened wills prevented the seasickness of the entire ship's company. It was half-past eleven before we passed the first bell-buoy. Half an hour later the wind died altogether, and we wallowed in a dead calm, while the booms banged impatiently from side to side, and the two mechanical logs (a German and an American, both second-hand and quite useless) which we were testing one against the other, hung perpendicularly like plummets in the sea. We had a rather hesitating luncheon, and then, at 2 p.m., the wind, which had taken no notice of my efforts on the accordion, gave us another little puff, in response, I believe, to my rendering of "Spanish Ladies" on the whistle. For two hours *Racundra* pointed north, and when we threw matches overboard she left them undeniably astern. At four we were in another desperate calm. At 5.30 I bathed and swam about the ship, with Riga Lighthouse still in sight bearing south, and the second buoy, the "howling buoy", ten miles out, bearing a little west of north. We had a few more slight puffs and then calm, then a few more puffs, and then, as the sun went down, a little land wind came out of the S.E. and carried us at 8.40 past the second buoy. We were now fairly at sea, and the wind holding, at 9.20 we boomed out a spare staysail as a spinnaker.

At ten o'clock the others turned in. For the first time not on paper and in dreams, I had the little ship alone in my hands in a night of velvet dark below and stars above, pushing steadily along into unknown waters. I was extremely happy. At midnight the wind swung round to the N.W., and for a moment I thought of calling up the Ancient to take the tiller while I shifted sails. Then I thought I might as well have a try by myself and call the others only if I could not help it. I lashed the tiller and handed the boomed staysail. Then with all the sheets in we were back again on our course, close-hauled now, and I was at the tiller listening anxiously to know if the others had heard my hurried running to and fro on deck. But if *Racundra* had been a sentient thing doing her best to help me, she could not have done more than she did. The whole operation had gone like clockwork, and the others had heard nothing, and did not know of the change in the wind or even of the wind's increase, until 4.30 a.m., when the Ancient came on deck and wondered what I had done with Riga light, which had seemed close aboard when he had gone down to his bunk.

During the night the binnacle light blew out again and again and finally refused to be relit. I steered by the North Star, which I kept bobbing about between the maintop and the peak. Our compass had not been adjusted, and a number of bearings I had taken on our way out had made it pretty clear that we had a lot of easterly deviation. Theoretically our course should have carried us eight or ten miles east of Runö. Practically I was sure that we should pass it much nearer, but, as the Ancient had small belief in deviation and said the compass was "right enough", I was prepared to try it out. After the Ancient came up and took the tiller I hung about the deck to see the dawn, which came up with fiery red splashes over a nickel sea. With the dawn the wind backed to the S.W., when we eased off the sheets, after which I went below and was instantly asleep.

At 7.30 I was waked by a feeling of excitement on board, and was told that Runö Island was in sight. I ran up on deck to see a low line of trees with a pale red lighthouse above them exactly over our bows. The easterliness of our compass was proved beyond a doubt, for even the Ancient could not suggest that we had been making leeway against the wind. But interest in this technical point was sunk in our delight at seeing this, the most romantic island in Northern Europe, at which we had so often looked on the chart that all summer had hung on the wall of my room. The spot on the chart, which long ago, sailing further north in *Slug* and in *Kittiwake*, we had so often promised ourselves to visit as soon as we should have a seaworthy ship, was becoming a reality before our eyes. I suppose most readers of this book have already lost the ecstatic joy of sighting land at sea. Yet, no. I do not believe that even for the oldest mariner that joy can ever fade. It is always new, always a miracle, never in the common ruck of absolutely predictable events. Islands especially stir the blood, and Runö, that lonely place, over fifty miles out from Riga and nearly as far from the Esthonian coast, with its Swedish seal-hunters using words that in Sweden have become archaic, living in the twentieth century a life of medieval communism, a place at which a steamer calls but once a year, coming up out of the sea before me, sought and found (however incorrectly) by my own little ship, gave me moments of unforgettable delight. The sunlight strengthened. The dark line seen through the binoculars became visible forest. The pale red tower began faintly to resemble the very inaccurate drawing

INHABITANTS OF RUNÖ.

of it which, as a guide to mariners, is tucked away into the drab mainland of the English charts of the Baltic. Under the forest appeared white lines and splashes, which the Ancient said were breakers but the glass showed to be sand. Then, as we came nearer, we could see the deserted beach and the broken-down wooden pier not to be visited by any steamer until July next year. There is anchorage off that pier in westerly winds, but it is unsafe if the wind blows on shore. Just now the anchorage was protected by the southern end of the island, and we steered directly for the pierhead. I took the tiller while the Ancient worked the lead, and we sent silent thanks to the *Baltabor* for lending it. "Three fathom," called the Ancient. "Two . . . Two and a half . . . Two . . . Two . . . Two and a half . . . One and a half . . ." Then down with the staysail, in with the sheets, round into the wind, and, as she began to go astern, "*Let go.*" The chain rattled slowly out and *Racundra*, pulling up to it, had found her first anchorage in foreign waters.

The wooden pier, which was in two pieces, the middle part of it having been washed away, was fifty or sixty yards from us. On the pierhead was a huge rusty anchor, a trophy from a wreck, or a keepsake from some vessel that had had to slip her cable because of some sudden change of wind and had not been able to come back and claim it before the islanders had fished it from the sea. Behind the pier lay sand-dunes, behind them enormous pines bigger than any I have seen even in the forests of Russia, and behind the trees the upper works of the lighthouse, an ugly structure of red iron tubes. The anchor and the lighthouse and the wrecked pier were the only things that spoke of man. The shore was deserted. There was not a human being to be seen. We sounded our fog-horn, thinking that maybe they would send out a boat. Nothing happened, and, half doubting if after all we had found the proper anchorage, we unlashed the dinghy, turned it over, and with the spare staysail halyards lowered it into the sea. The Cook and I tumbled in and pulled ashore. The wind showed signs of changing, and we knew that if it veered farther to the south we should have to be off again without delay.

Our landing on Runö was like a page from *Robinson Crusoe* or a child's dream of desert islands. We rowed in past the broken end of pier and, in shallow water, tied up to the rotting timbers of the part of it that ran out from the land. We climbed up and, stepping carefully over the crazy planking came to the sandy shore. Hummocks of sand rose before us, but north and south of the strip of sand we could see rocks out in the water. And there, almost on the edge of this tideless sea, were those gigantic pine-trees, growing out of a thick mossy carpet rich with brown and scarlet mushrooms. On a pair of rough wheels made of solid wood without spokes rested one end of a felled tree roughly trimmed. But as we went in under those tremendous arches of the forest there was an uncanny absence of any human sound. The sand dunes hid the pier. The towering trees hid the iron lighthouse. There was nothing but the green-carpeted forest, cloisters for giants, and that great trunk on wheels exactly like those that must have been made by the first wheelwright in the history of our race. Man, should he appear, might be of any kind. Almost, we looked up in the treetops for pigmies with their poisoned arrows, and watched the trunks of the trees for the feathers of one of Fenimore Cooper's Indian braves.

And then, slowly wandering towards us, knocking off the heads of the mushrooms with his stick, came man indeed, the Governor-General of the Island, a short, lame, elderly man in blue canvas clothes and a seaman's cap, the keeper of the lighthouse, to whom the men of Runö come for a casting vote in all debates. He has no official authority; no laws confer power on him or limit it; but . . . he is the Keeper of the Light, the guardian of the one piece of civilization imposed on Runö by the mainland, the representative of those who do not live on islands, and, I suppose, tradition invests him with a sort of dignity. In old days he was sent by a Tsar of Russia to keep the light of this little island in a sea surrounded on all sides by Russian territory. The men of Runö are Swedes, and a Tsar of Russia had driven their race from the mainland. But nowadays the sea of which Runö is as it were the central pole is no longer Russian. Its coasts are Latvian and Esthonian. The Tsar is no more, and the Swedes of Runö can hardly think with any great humility of the two little nations which argue, fairly bitterly, as to which of them should really own the island on which, indifferent to such politics, the Swedes live on, preserving their own life and their own customs in an odd kind of private Middle Ages, centuries removed from the modern competitive struggle of the continent.

The lighthouse-keeper greeted us. He had heard our foghorn, and since the people were busy with their harvesting on the other side of the island had himself come down to meet us, and to warn us that the wind was changing and that we must soon look to our ship. He knew a few words of English, but more willingly spoke Russian, which he knew well, besides, of course, Estonian and Swedish. He was surprised to see us so late in the year, and, on learning my nationality, asked with the embarrassing curiosity of foreigners to whom this bit of our mingled foreign and domestic affairs is always hard to explain, "Well, Mister, and how is it with Ireland?" This was the first of several such disappointments, for I had hoped in voyaging among these remote islands to be quit of politics for once. But I hid my feelings and told him that the Irish were settling their affairs in the Irish way, and then got him to talk of his own country.

I knew already that on Runö competition is almost unknown. Instead there is a sort of ancient communism. The men of Runö are seal-hunters, and at a later stage of our cruise we met some of them actually at their work. Each seal killed belongs not to the lucky hunter but to the community as a whole. The land has been divided into workable farms, and if a family increases it cannot acquire fresh land. It merely adds the necessary room space to the farmhouse, and often does not even do that. If a son marries, he builds himself a bed, which is set up in the room of his parents, and twenty years later, if his son marries and the grandparents are still alive, another bed is built. You can number the families in a Runö house by counting the double beds in the main room. There are two hundred and seventy persons on the island. The women wear on holidays the national costume of old Sweden. Coming out of church on Sundays (they are devout Lutherans) they are as uniform as a procession of nuns. The men wear homespun clothes and sealskin shoes. Their morals are said to be strict. I have heard that some years ago a woman offended against their code, whereupon they tried her by general assembly and condemned her to death. It was found, however, that not one of them was willing to kill her. So they fastened her in the bottom of a little old boat and set her adrift in a storm. The boat did not sink, but was thrown upon the Courland coast, and the woman, still alive, was found by fishermen, recovered, and, one is left to suppose, continued her wicked career on the mainland, where people are less critical.

The lighthouse-keeper told us that people were beginning to take an interest in Runö; that this year the steamer had brought them Mr. Piip, the Esthonian Foreign Minister, and a very great Englishman (our own Minister from Riga), but that these events did not much affect the islanders, who had never considered themselves Russians, nor indeed anything else than men of Runö, and were content to remain so, and to be counted Esthonian, seeing that their business, when they had any, was with Arensburg; that they caught their seals on the Esthonian rocks, and that, after all, the lighthouse-keeper had always been sent from Reval. He took us with him to see his lighthouse, where he posed for his photograph very nobly with the lighthouse behind him. It had been higher, he said, but the Germans had blown off the top of it, besides making a horrible mess of his house. Civilization had visited Runö after all. At the lighthouse we had a drink of fresh water, and then, as the wind shifted definitely to the south, had to give up all thoughts of staying longer on the island, and hurried away over the thick moss under the gigantic trees, picking mushrooms as we went, and so to the broken-down pier.

We were none too soon. *Racundra* was bobbing up and down in a manner undignified for her, and the Ancient had lowered the peak. Where the water had been smooth it was already broken. We pulled out in the dinghy, getting well splashed on the way, hauled it on board, got our anchor, hoisted the staysail, filled on the starboard tack, and were off for Paternoster and the entrance to the Moon Sound.

RUNÖ TO PATERNOSTER

It was half-past one when we got away, and, as we were anxious to take no chances with the rocks on Runö's northern corner, we sailed due east for a mile before putting *Racundra* on her course. I must point out here that until we reached Helsingfors, though our courses were duly set by compass, there was very considerable discrepancy between theory and practice. After the Runö landfall I allowed a full point for easterly deviation in the neighbourhood of north, and this proved to be about right when, in Finland, we had magnets put in and swung the ship. But on other points the error was even greater. Our logs also were of small use for navigation. Of the two, the German log did not work at all, and the American, which we used, was a most pessimistic affair. Unless we were going at our top speed in half a gale, it registered a little less than two thirds of the distance we actually covered, and, if we were not visibly and sensibly churning along, the log seemed to lose heart altogether and registered nothing at all. I think it had begun life on a motorboat and had no patience with our old-fashioned but superior ways. Its remarks were of use only in giving us the roughest ideas as to what we had been doing.

The wind was now S.S.W. but continued to back to the south, and at 3.40 we brought the booms over. It was a fine day and pleasant sailing, and, whatever the log might say, it was clear enough from our own wake that we were steadily moving towards the Esthonian coast. The only question in our minds was where we were going to hit it and when. We did a lot of straightening up on board, drank coffee by the pint, and ate huge quantities of food. We were all greatly cheered by our speed after the dismal experience of yesterday's calms, and the

Ancient began to think we should be in Reval tomorrow and to talk of record passages.

"One time," said he – "one time I crossed the North Sea in twenty-four hours under sail."

"Where was that?" I asked. "Harwich to the Hook?"

"No," said he, with a sail-needle between his teeth, finishing the end of one of the halyards. "It was from that place up at the North of Scotland . . . like the Moon Sund, where we're going."

"Pentland Firth?"

"Ay. Pentland. Twenty-four hours from there to the Norwegian coast."

"Pretty good sailing."

"And I had my captain sick all the way. Yellow fever. That was how it was. We were in Mexico when he began ill, and I wanted him to go ashore. But he was Norwegian, and he would have it that back to Norway would put him right. And I thought myself, 'Maybe the fresh airs at sea will put the fever under.' But it was not like that. Every day he grew worse. I wanted to put up into one of the American ports to put him ashore, but he wouldn't have it, and was all for carrying on and getting home to Norway. And we did carry on, too. I can't tell you how long we were on the passage, but we had a west wind with us all the way, till we were near the Irish coast. I wanted them to put through the Channel, and let him see a doctor at Southampton, or one of them places. But he wouldn't have it, and, sick as he was, set a course round by the north of Scotland. ' Tis the best way for Norway,' he says. And we came through the Pentland Firth, and he was so bad that I was for hauling our wind and coming to Aberdeen. But he would have nothing of it. And the west wind held and plenty of it, and the captain in his fever shouting, whenever I spoke to him, not to take a foot of canvas off her. And we made the Norwegian coast in twenty-four hours. And then we went into Christiansund, where he was from, and as soon as the anchor was down he went ashore, and as he went I told him I'd come ashore and see him in the morning. But it was not like that. I never saw him again, for he died during the night."

I had set a course that, if the error of the compass was about what it seemed to be, should bring *Racundra* within sight of the well-lit coast to the west of the Paternoster Lighthouse, so that we might learn our exact position in plenty of time, and was consequently delighted when at 10.15 we picked up a blinking light on the starboard bow. The Ancient took the tiller while I ran down below for a stop-watch. I timed it. One flash every three seconds. I looked at the chart which I had spread out on the writing-table in the cabin. No such light was to be found upon it. I looked again all along the coast of Oesel. No. There was a four-flash light on Laiduninna and nothing else between that and Paternoster. I ran my finger across the chart, which I was lighting with a little electric pocket-lamp. Away to west, far out of our supposed course, near the approach of Arensburg, a blinking light was marked, but the period of its flashes was not named. If it were that, then how humbled must be the pride of the navigator. I could feel the Ancient waiting in the dark to hear me, having timed the light by a method (the stop-watch) in which he did not believe, admit that I did not know what light it was or where we might be. It was a most unpleasant moment. So I said nothing at all.

"What course?" asked the Ancient.

"E.N.E.," said I, to give myself time. I had just remembered that there was yet hope for my navigation. We were working by the big German chart of 1915, the only comparatively large-scale chart I had been able to get. But in the chart case was an English small-scale chart covering the Riga Gulf as well as much else, and this had been corrected up to the spring of this year. I pulled it out and spread it on the folding-table under the lamp in the cabin. And, as I looked from yellow splash to yellow splash (lights are marked in this way) going from west to east along the Oesel coast, behold, the very last light on that coast before the light of Paternoster at the entrance to the Sound was marked "1 flash ev. 3 sec.", with the date "1920". My expanding joy almost lifted off the cabin roof. I went on deck again a different man from that cringing, worried navigator who was glad that the dark hid the doubt in his face. For some few minutes I said nothing. Then, with all the ease I could assume, I said lightly, as if it were nothing: "Keep a look out for a flashing light on the starboard bow." By changing our course we had brought my first treasure trove to port, "And then," I added, "we should find another light to port, with a white flash every second; and when that turns to red, we shall have our course clear for the entrance."

The Ancient answered not a word, but there was a new warmth in the night air, a new solidity in the floor of the steering-well, and various other minor indications of rewarded confidence. I went below and smoked a most satisfactory pipe.

We were not moving fast, and it was three hours later before we had the other two lights. But I was secretly glad we were moving slowly because, confidence or no confidence, I did not want to try too much and attempt the Moon Sound in the dark. In spite of the evidence of the English chart, I was glad enough to have our course confirmed by meeting at 3 a.m. a steamer going S.W., which I knew must have come out of the Sound. I took the hint and altered our course a little accordingly. A little later, the white light of Paternoster turned red and then our last doubts were gone, and, as the dawn rose, and with it the wind strengthened from the S.E., we found ourselves exactly in the entrance to the Sound, Paternoster Lighthouse on its island on our port, Werder on our starboard bow, islands and rocky coast stretching away behind us to the south and west, and before us the Sound itself.

THROUGH THE MOON SOUND

THE actual entrance to the Sound is a couple of miles wide, with the little island of Virelaid on the western side and the larger mass of Werder on the eastern, each with its lighthouse. Then, though in some parts of it the shores recede and in places are over twenty miles apart, the actual channel narrows, twists and turns with such sharpness that big ships have more than once gone aground through attempting a corner too fast or at a time when the current was too strong against them. I suppose there are few sections of sea chart on which so many wrecks are marked. There is, of course, no tide, but the water rises and falls according to the prevailing winds, which also determine the direction of the strong current in the narrows. The Russian battleship *Slava* is still to be seen high out of water on the Kumora Shoal. The British merchantman *Toledo*, after three years of waiting, was only last autumn hauled off the shoal by the Erik Stone. Few British skippers care to attempt the passage by night, and one of the most careful, who did so venture, lost several plates from his ship's bottom as his reward.

We, of course, were attempting it by day, and, as dawn broke and at 5.30 we had Paternoster Lighthouse abeam, the wind strengthened mightily from the south, and, from the slant of the spar-buoys, we could see that we had not only the wind but also a strong current with us. We had the most favourable possible conditions. At the same time, I was not going to take any risks on *Racundra's* maiden trip. With our shallow draught we could, no doubt, have cut off many corners. We draw, even with the centreboard down, no more than seven and a half feet. Our good friend *Baltabor*, on her way to Reval from Riga, avoids the Sound and goes round outside the islands if she draws over

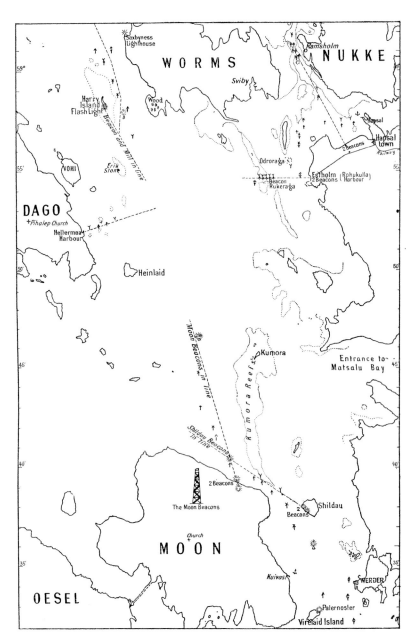

CHART OF MOON SOUND.

fourteen feet. I decided to attribute fourteen feet to the modest, the admirable *Racundra*, and pilot her through exactly as if she were a big ship. In this way we should have ample margin for the correction of any errors due to eccentricities of current or the like.

Passing Paternoster, we opened Kuivast on the island of Moon, a little anchorage where there is a landing-stage, a coastguard station, an inn and a telegraph. I had meant to stop there an hour or two, but the conditions for passing the Sound were so good that I visited Kuivast only through the binoculars. Two or three schooners were at anchor there, waiting for a favourable wind to take them south. The inn looked tempting enough, but, there it was: that glum log of ours was spinning merrily as a top, the sun was bright, the wind fair and strong, the wooded island of Shildau showed ahead, through the glasses I could already see one of the pair of beacons that, kept in line over our stern, would guide us through the next bit of the channel; after all, there were plenty of stopping-places ahead, and we could visit Kuivast homeward bound. So I put the island of Moon resolutely aside and looked over the bows at Shildau, and searched the pale blue, windswept water before us for a bell-and-light buoy, which I presently found. *Racundra* foamed past it, and I brought it in line over her stern with the lighthouse on Sareots Point, the western end of Werder. The sun shone, the wind blew, and there was the second beacon on Shildau, at first hard to see, close down on the shore under a background of dark-green pines. And then Shildau was abeam, then on our quarter, and behold, that dimly discerned second beacon grew clearer, separated itself from the trees, stood out, moved slowly nearer and nearer, close to, and at last was in line with the first. Up to starboard with the helm, over with the booms, and off goes *Racundra*, with those two beacons in line over her stern, through the narrowest stretch of channel, a lane between the shoals close by the N.E. corner of the island of Moon. And there, sure enough, on the low green ridge of that island, seeming at first to be in impossible positions, but straightening themselves out as we sped along, were two tall beacons of open ironwork, fantastic, unmistakable things, each with a dark iron corkscrew or snake twisting from the top to bottom in a narrow iron cage. Woods, windmills, green pastureland, houses, and those beacons, looking like Mr. Wells's monsters from another planet striding over the earth, all changed places in a vast quadrille as *Racundra* hurried on her way. Suddenly the two monsters began noticeably to draw nearer to each other. They were within shouting distance of each other. They were in close converse. They were one. The corkscrew of one monster linked with the corkscrew of the other, the two cages merged into a single cage, and then, to port with the helm and sharply, and *Racundra*, shaking the waters from her beloved nose, was off again almost at right-angles from her former course, while the Shildau beacons slid rapidly apart, and this new pair remained in magic unity. I took a bearing on the Moon beacons and compared it with the chart, and got additional confirmation of the error I had assumed from our Runö landfall. That was at ten minutes past eight in the morning, and the log was reading 38.4. Half an hour later it was reading 41.6, so that even its pessimism was compelled to admit that *Racundra* was doing her six knots.

We were now in apparently open water, but the chart was of a different opinion, and, mindful of our temporary fourteen feet, we kept those beacons in line for seven miles, when we passed the light-buoy in the middle of the Sound. Away to the west was the wide shallow inland sea between the islands of Dagö and Oesel. To the east we could see small scraps of islets and knew that beyond them was the narrow bay of Matsalu, from which, more than seven hundred years ago, the Esthonians sailed out and away to Sweden, and burnt Sigtuna, the Swedish capital, and carried away its silver gates. After passing the light-buoy, we held on our course for another seven miles or so, when we sighted the murderous Erik Stone, a square rock sticking up alone out of the waters; a rock no bigger than a king's throne, as it is said by some to have been; a rock painted red all over by my ingenious friend Captain Konga, with whom, as you shall hear in another place, I spent two nights on the wreck of the *Toledo*, aground upon the shoal of which this stone is the uppermost point. Then, the water had been lower, and there was a little island to be seen, and seabirds upon it, but now there was nothing but the stone itself. Far away to the west was the coast of Dagö, and, with strong glasses, we could see the white house and a red roof by the little harbour of Heltermaa. Far away to the east a fantastic iron beacon rose out of the sea, showing where was the narrow passage to Hapsal between the shoals of Odroraga and Rukeraga. We meant to return that way, but we were moving too fast to have time to spare for dreaming about passages to come. There was the Erik Stone; there on the starboard bow the dark woods of the island of Worms; there, as if floating in the sea, the handful of low buildings on the tiny island of Harry; and somewhere ahead another bell-buoy to be found and passed to make the channel along the eastern side of Harry and avoid the rocks off Worms.

The sun shone; the wind blew stronger and stronger; short, stout little waves raced us, caught us, passed foaming and gurgling under our keel and rushed ahead of us to the open Baltic. We were off Worms almost before we had left the Erik Stone, so it seemed. And there sheltering under the wooded island of Worms were the vessels bound south, schooners and cutters at anchor, watching us with envy as we flew past, waiting for the wind to change that was no good to them and suited us so well. Worms, like Runö, is one of the Swedish islands belonging to Esthonia. In all the harbours along the coasts of this part of the Baltic you meet stout little ships with Swedish names and the words "fran Wormsö" painted on their broad sterns. You can tell a Worms ship at first sight. You have no need to seek the painted letters. No others have the same combination of beam and lofty freeboard fore and aft. A beautiful sheer these little ships have, with a high afterdeck, the sides of which tumble home with an effect no less practical than lovely – a downward curve to the broad midships and then a proud upward sweep to the bows; in every line the sense of solidity, breadth, ability to keep the seas, and an unbroken tradition of simple-minded builders.

The ships are mostly iron-fastened nowadays, but the older art is preserved, and I have seen fine schooners, not more than five years old, in which the fastenings, like timbers and planking, were of wood. For a moment we thought to turn aside, to slip in here under the lee of the island, to make this a stage of our journey and to talk with some of the little anchored fleet. But what would a Worms skipper think of us if we wasted a fair wind? It was not yet noon and the wind showed signs of rising still more. The barometer had fallen and was still falling. The wind would hold, and, going at this speed, we should be in Reval before midnight. So Worms slipped astern and we held on out into the Baltic, still among shoals, but with nothing visible on either hand except the glaucous white-splashed water.

WORMS TO PAKERORT

For some time we steered north by west through a waste of water increasingly disturbed, looking south over *Racundra's* stern and keeping a dark pinewood promontory on the south end of Worms just open of the slim, gleaming white tower of Saxbiness light on the N.W. corner of the island. The wind, now really blowing pretty hard, kept shifting, and more than once we had to jibe. We passed one spar-buoy, then another, then found the long expected light-buoy, and north of that a group of four spar-buoys and a solitary pair.

Spar-buoys are the loneliest things in the sea. For those who do not know them I should perhaps have said before that they are tall posts anchored to the bottom of the sea to mark the shallows. On their ends in these parts they carry brooms, one or two, and according to the number of the brooms and to their position, the handles of the brooms being up or down, the mariner learns on which side of the buoy is the danger. The brooms do not long survive the buffeting of wind and water, and these lone sticks with their draggle-tailed besoms far out at sea have a most melancholy appearance in themselves, although the sailor finding his way over the waters is glad enough to recognize them and be assured of his position. We rushed past that solitary pair, jibed for the last time, and stood away E.N.E. for the narrow passage across the reef that almost joins Odensholm to Spithamn.

The wind strengthened in successive stout breaths, and then settled down in the S.E., to blow considerably harder than *Racundra* had yet had opportunity of feeling. We were some eight or ten miles off the land, and the wind, blowing since the

afternoon of yesterday, had had plenty of time to get up the
waves – nothing, of course, compared to those there must
have been on the other side of the Gulf, but still enough to
make a pretty fair test of *Racundra's* quality. With her broad
beam and heavy keel she stood up to the wind magnificently,
of course, but, as she dropped between each wave, something
fairly thundered within her, shaking the whole ship. It was the
centreboard, and we hauled it up, for, with the wind broad on
her beam and plenty of it, the difference it made to her sailing
(if any, for she is by no means flat-bottomed) was fully
discounted by the pounding effect on our nerves. Even so we
were left with a noise to which to grow accustomed – the
tremendous crashing of the water under her weather bilge keel
as she sank into the trough. As soon as we knew what it was,
we stopped worrying, but before we knew we had crawled all
over inside her, feeling her sides, inspecting the boltheads
of her three-and-a-half-ton keel, and generally expecting
unpleasant surprises. Once we knew what it was, it rapidly
became unnoticeable, and we were able whole-heartedly to
rejoice in *Racundra's* manner of dealing with waves, a thing
beautiful to see. We took plenty of spray on deck, but no
heavy water at all. "She juist joomps out of them like
a dinghy," said the Ancient, restored to happiness after doubts,
during the centreboard's orchestral performances, as to
whether the keel was adrift. In the general buffeting she
got between leaving the Moon Sound and coming into
shelter of the land by Spithamn, only one thing gave way.
In the working drawings for her there had been a neat
galvanized iron saddle and ring by way of gaff jaws, but the
builder, saving money, had not bought it, and, at the last
minute, had made wooden jaws, with holes for the lacing
bored far too big, thereby weakening a contraption which
even apart from that was rather ineffectively held together
with screws. Further, the shrouds of the mainmast fell rather
far aft, and the mainsail being very tall, the gaff tended to
swing forward and press against the shroud, putting an unfair
strain on the jaws. We had heard a loud crack aloft, but
nothing had come down, and from the steering-well we could

see no damage. After sighting the low island of Odensholm with its lighthouse, and finding the two buoys that mark the passage just north of the promontory of Spithamn, where more ships were taking refuge under the lee of the rising ground with its six windmills, we heard another crack. I set a course to take us north of Sandgrund and the rocks beyond Spithamn, left the tiller to the Ancient, and went forward to take a look at things. I saw at once that the parrel rings of the gaff jaws were hanging loose, that the gaff jaws were broken, and that the broken side of the jaws was jammed in place by a halyard, which, bar-taut, was the only thing that kept the gaff from breaking loose. This was pretty unpleasing, but, after watching it for a minute or two, I became convinced that nothing would shift it so long as we held the wind on the starboard side, which we should do until we came to Reval Bay. In any case we were moving finely, and this place, with Sandgrund, Grasgrund and the Locust Rock all to be avoided, was not the one to choose for a stoppage for repairs.

We held on, and *Racundra*, settling down to her work, justified our trust by the speed with which she hurried eastwards. At 6.5 we had Grasgrund abeam and saw the lonely rock, well out to sea, where in fine weather there is often a broad space of visible ground. On our starboard bows were the islands of Roogö, off which we had been becalmed one summer's night in *Kittiwake*. There was Pakerort Lighthouse, tall on its cliff, the witness of how many of our struggles in the recalcitrant but lamented *Slug*. In the bay on the higher side of Pakerort was Baltic Port. We were already in familiar waters. And, with the thought of Baltic Port, our pleasant anchorage of last summer, came doubts as to the wisdom of standing on for Reval in the dark through what in any other boat we should have called a storm, with so serious a piece of trouble as broken gaff jaws awaiting attention aloft. We should have to beat into Reval Bay anyhow, when the gaff jaws would infallibly come down. It would then be dark. Better beat into Roogowik, to Baltic Port, here, now, in daylight, when, if anything went wrong, we could see what we were about. So, rather nervously, we hauled in the sheets, put the helm down for a moment, and stood close-hauled into Roogowik. But we were already too late. The deep bay running S.E. into the land left us again without protection, we were bucketing into a head sea, *Racundra's* speed fell off, and the twilight was upon us. It became imperative to have a look at those gaff jaws while it was yet light enough to see. The Ancient lowered away the peak, which stuck, of course, in the makeshift blocks, then loosed the throat halyard, when the whole thing came down in a tumultuous and entangled rush. Within a minute we had learned that with her staysail and mizen setting as badly as they then were, *Racundra* would have a very difficult time beating against a heavy sea under those two sails alone. She absolutely refused to stay (I hasten to explain that now, since we have put things right and given her the tackle she deserves, after generally clearing up the abounding errors in her rigging, she stays with the utmost regularity). We had to wear her each time we went about. Now, Roogowik is a narrow inlet deep to either shore, but with rocks along both sides and an awkward reef running out north of the harbour, which is well into the inlet on the eastern side. It grew perfectly dark. The harbour lights appeared, but there were no lights whatever on the Roogö island shore opposite the harbour. We could not tell how near we were to the land when on the tack that took us in that direction. The wind was extremely strong (indeed, if it had been weaker our position would perhaps have been worse); our sidelights would not burn, and the binnacle light blew out every time it was lit. We found ourselves not snugly making repairs in Baltic Port, as we had hoped, but rushing wildly in the dark from one side to the other of the bay, desperately wearing round when we thought we could afford to go no farther, and gaining absolutely nothing in our struggle towards the green light which meant, as I thought then, a well-known harbour.

Providence, perhaps, was with us, for, as we were to learn a fortnight later, if we had gone in there with the wind behind us, as it would have been if only we could have made the entrance, which is from the south, we should almost certainly have been smashed up. The harbour had been halved in size since last year. The open space through which I should have tried to go to my old anchorage had been blocked by a new pier of black tarred timbers, quite invisible at night, and my old anchorage, behind it, was high and dry out of the water. I do not like to think of what would have happened if, with that wind, we had raced into that blind alley in the dark.

However, we had no chance of doing any such thing. With the darkness the wind increased to a gale and our position became rather seriously uncomfortable, for it became clear that, so far from gaining, we were actually losing ground, and that with each tack we were coming nearer to the reef instead of farther into the bay beyond it. At this point, the Ancient and I had our only quarrel. He wanted to get as near the harbour mouth as we could, drop anchor and try to get a line ashore. I knew the place well from other years, and so knew that the depth was far too great to give us a chance of doing anything but lose an anchor, and that if we got anywhere near the shore, unless actually in the harbour mouth, we should infallibly go on a rock. I was therefore for admitting that Baltic Port was a mistake, for wearing for the last time, getting well out into the middle of the bay and clear of the reef, and then putting the helm up and running out to sea until beyond the precipitous point of Pakerort, when I should bring her up to the wind and remain so till morning. There was a little breathless bitterness on the subject as we shouted at each other and tried to hear what the other was shouting back, and it ended in *Racundra* pretending she had never wanted to put her nose into Baltic Port at all. She stopped bucketing into the wind, and with sudden restfulness and three times the speed, flew out of the bay with the wind at her heels to the open sea, where she was more at home. The Ancient watched Pakerort light till from the cliff-top it looked down over our stern, and then went below and to sleep. There was, after all, nothing more to be done.

PAKERORT TO REVAL

THEN began a wild but, in a curious way, rather enjoyable night. No misfortunes at sea are enjoyable in themselves. He is a liar who says they are and he is a fool who courts them. But when misfortune has come against your will, when it is there, when you have shaken hands with it, realized it thoroughly, and done what you think is the best possible thing to do, there comes a sort of release from further worry which is quite sensibly pleasant.

There was *Racundra* with her mainsail gone, proved incapable of beating under staysail and mizen, rigged as they then were in a temporary manner, careering through steep seas in a pitch-dark night with no sidelights and a binnacle lamp that would not burn. On the face of it, misery. Yet there was no misery about it. While in that narrow bay I had been much afraid, but here, in the open sea, things were better. Besides, we were doing the thing which I had myself urged as the right thing to do. It was my own thing, this careering business out here in the dark, and I had the joy of possession. I was still afraid, of course, but knew where I was, and knew what I had to avoid. I had to prevent *Racundra* from being blown too far out to sea, to prevent her from working sideways to Nargon island, and to make headway if possible towards the shallow bay on this side of Surop, without going on the rocks off the near point of it and without getting into the bay until it was light enough to see what we were about. Wind and sea had clearly made up their minds to knock us and blow us to Finland, or, if we insisted on working sideways, to plant us on Nargon like many good ships before us. *Racundra* and I were of a different determination, and, as we careered in the dark over waves which always seem bigger at night, I had the definite impression that *Racundra* was enjoying it also in her fashion. I found myself, who do not sing in happier moments, yelling "Spanish Ladies" and "Summer is icumen in" and "John Peel" at the top of my voice. Then the Cook struggled up the companion-way with a sandwich. She asked, with real inquiry, "Are we going to be drowned before morning?"

I leaned forward from the steering-well and shouted, "Why?"

"Because I have two thermos flasks full of hot coffee. If we are, we may as well drink them both. If not, I'll keep one till tomorrow."

We kept one. We drank the hot coffee from the other and ate a huge quantity of sandwiches. The more we ate the better things seemed. We grew accustomed even to the din. Douses of spray merely made it seem worth while to have put on oilskins. The howling of the wind and the recurrent crashing of the waters became monotonous. The Cook, who had been doing her work as calmly as *Racundra*, and like *Racundra* was enjoying it, fell asleep in the middle of a laugh. She was tired out, and when the next big splash woke her, I sent her below to lie down, knowing that there would be plenty of work for her in the morning, whereas there was nothing she could well do at the moment. I do not believe she has forgiven me yet.

After that, Pakerort light and Surop light and the faraway flash of Nargon were my companions. The riding light, the only one of our lamps that would burn except the swinging lamp in the cabin, I had under my knees in the steering-well. With an electric pocket-lamp I had a look at the binnacle now and again. So we went on, hour after hour, until I too fell asleep.

I suppose everybody who has spent long hours at the tiller of a little boat has done the same. But, I admit, I was startled the first time I woke to find myself in the steering-well of *Racundra*, holding a kicking tiller, with the dark in my eyes and a great wind in my face. The next time it happened I said to myself, "Done it again!" and began pinching myself as hard as I could, in muscles, in any places that seemed to hurt, in the effort to keep awake. It was no use. The lamp was burning all night in the cabin and light came up through the round windows in the cabin roof. I had shifted the riding light from the floor of the steering-well to the seat behind me. A faint divided light was thrown on the staysail and the upturned shape of the dinghy lashed underneath it on the foredeck, and these in successive dreams took different shapes. I found myself wrestling with a large and difficult collar-stud stuck in a stiff shirt, and only slowly came to understand that the collar-stud was the tiller and the white shirt spreading somewhere before me was the lonely staysail. A minute or two later the dinghy was the moulded base of a huge table and the staysail was a corner of a tablecloth most annoyingly put on crooked. "Do put that cloth straight," I woke saying, and found myself, as before, keeping *Racundra* up into the wind.

I think that is the secret. One could not go to sleep at the tiller with the wind aft, but, when close-hauled, steering is done so much by feel, especially in the dark, that the ship takes care of the sleeping helmsman. I never once woke with sails flapping, and never once to find that I had fallen off the wind. *Racundra* took care of her skipper, who was far too tired to take care of himself. Then, suddenly, the sleeping fit passed from me and I was extraordinarily awake, most unpleasantly aware of what I took to be some martial idiot rushing about with a little ship of war showing no lights but the occasional disconcerting flash of a projector. Then came the lights of a steamer from the west (as I learnt afterwards, our old friend the *Baltabor* from Riga), also at that time, when we were bucketing about without sidelights, a thing of infinite hate. And then, suddenly, with a relief which let me know how great the strain had been, I knew that the eastern sky was distinguishable from the sea. Day was coming at last, and with day the possibility of doing more than hold our own, if indeed we had been doing that.

Day came, or the light before the day, and I found exultantly that I was now not sleepy at all. We had done much better than I had expected in the dark. We were well clear of Nargon and about two miles from Surop. I held on joyfully, no longer thinking of calling the Ancient, who at last, when the sun was up, came on deck and, with that little faith of his, as once before he had looked for Riga, now looked for Pakerort. Everything was hope. We could see what we were doing, and the Ancient dug out the trysail from the solid mass of gear and sails stowed in the forecastle during our hurried departure. We disentangled a halyard and got the trysail up, wore ship after an ineffectual attempt to go about, and stood in on the port tack for Fall and the hollow of the broad bay west of Surop, to get under the shelter of the land for repairs that would let us hoist the mainsail again, without which we were so badly crippled. At last we got into fairly smooth water. We drank the hot coffee from that other thermos flask. The Cook worked one of her miracles and produced great bowls of porridge. The Ancient Mariner made a wonderful job of a manila rope substitute for gaff jaws. This done, the Cook took the tiller while we took off the trysail and hoisted the main. Would it stand or would it not? It stood most beautifully, and with singing hearts we went about on the starboard tack, cleared the rocks by Surop and then, coming nearer to the wind, held on till close by Cape Basanova, the S.E. point of Nargon, where, long before, we had landed on our first voyage in *Slug*. Then we went about and stood due south, the wind having momentarily backed to the east. We stood into Zigelsko Bay. Reval was in sight for a moment, then blotted out by big rain-squalls. We went about thinking to clear Karlo, but the wind shifted too, and had such strength that even with eased mizen it took all the strength I had to keep her off the point, which she seemed determined to ram. I ran her off a little whenever I got a chance, but there were moments when it was impossible to do anything but luff, and Karlo, now and again invisible in the squalls, seemed most unpleasantly close. These squalls were, I think, the toughest wind we had throughout the storm, and *Racundra*, forced over by them, and meeting the short steep waves of the entrance to Reval Bay, shipped more water than throughout the whole of the rest of the passage. The Ancient had left the forecastle hatch open under the overturned dinghy, and until the Cook, guessing what had happened, went forward and closed it from underneath, each wave that came over sent a deluge below. Holding on in the cabin in a sort of whirlwind of flying pots, pans, apples, pipes and other loose lumber, the Cook was persuaded we were going to run her bodily under water, but *Racundra's* admirable nose took care of that. We had a wet but exhilarating time clearing Karlo, after which the squalls slackened, and we stood right across the bay towards the low hill and windmill by Miderando, went about there, and tacking with long legs and short, made our way up the bay towards the three ships of the Esthonian Grand Fleet and the rock and spires of Reval, dim in the rain, with each tack getting more into shelter and finding things easier, until at last we rounded smoothly into the harbour, picked up a buoy, warped into a berth by the Yacht Club mole, made all snug and had a pretty decisive supper.

PORT OF REVAL

I suppose it is as true as many things in history that Linda, with whom Esthonian chronicles begin, was born from a grouse's egg. She refused the sun and the moon in marriage, giving them the soundest categorical reasons for their rejection, and married instead the young giant Kalev, who, after a seven days' wedding feast, drove off with her in his sledge and came to this wild country by the seashore. Their son, the Kalevipoeg after whom the Esthonians name their ships, cleared parts of the country from rocks and made places fit for corn-growing and pasture, slew all the wild beasts, took part in the struggles of his people against the Christian invaders from Germany, and ended in hell with his fist stuck fast in the doorpost thereof. The old giant Kalev died here at Reval, and Linda heaped stone after stone upon his grave and so made that proud hill of Reval by the Baltic Sea, to carry in stone and mortar the record of over seven hundred years of Esthonian history. Up there on the skyline are fortifications built by the Danes. There are walls and towers built by the Swedes. The old town hall under the shadow of the rock is a legacy from the Hanseatic League. There is the ancient Lutheran church with the skeleton carved by the doorway. There are the narrow houses of the German merchants, some of them with the old portraits of the burghers still on the walls; up on the hill-top the houses of the barons, and over all the monstrous gold-domed Russian church, breaking with a touch of Byzantium the Gothic and Scandinavian outlines of the place. But for the Russian church, Reval is in colour a little like Shaftesbury; in form its rock is a little like the rock of Edinburgh, if only that were set in a plain on the edge of the sea. Most of all, it is like those night-cap-country towns that the old German wood-engravers used to put into their backgrounds.

But I know Reval too well, and like it too much, to be able to write of it with the aloof ease that is only possible in writing of chance acquaintanceships with towns and people. Sailing in there is always, for me, like coming home, and I hardly know how to give a picture of it as if I were seeing it for the first time.

Coming in as we did on this occasion in a series of rain-squalls, there was little of the town to be seen; but going home to the hills a man does not feel their presence the less if the tops are veiled in clouds. Everything in the harbour was an old friend. There were the little tugs, the *Kalev* and the *Walter*. How often their wash had almost rolled me off the roof of *Kittiwake's* cabin, on which I used to sit here in the evenings watching the ships! There was the old grey elevator that somehow, though modern, carries with it a suggestion of Danzig and the Hansa towns, rising high above us amid a forest of masts, for the basin beside it was full of schooners and cutters. Beside the quays were the little steamships *Ebba Munck* and *Kalevipoeg*, busy as usual on their regular trips to Finland and Stockholm. The same old motor-boat on the Yacht Club Quay was undergoing the same old repairs, and even the buoy to which we made fast was one into which I had often bumped in bringing the erratic *Kittiwake* home at night. Why, *Kittiwake* herself, unkempt, dilapidated, lovable little thing, was moored just on the other side of the mole.

The stranger going ashore for the first time at Reval from his little ship need ask no other guide than the castle rock. Leaving the harbour, he has but to follow the road that leads towards the hill and he will enter the town as it should be entered, through an old stone gateway defended by a tower, with stout and lofty stone walls stretching to right and left. He will then walk on a cobbled street or on a very narrow pavement under ancient houses until he comes to the foot of the rock. He can then climb by a zigzag path up the face of the cliff, but if he is wise, and would not spoil what is before him by preliminary tastes, he will keep on under the walls till, through a narrow street, he comes to another fortified gateway, and going through that will climb a long slope within the inner wall until he comes by the fantastic Russian church to the upper town, as it is called, built on the summit of the fortress. Here is the old house of the Russian Governor, where the Esthonian Parliament meets. Still working upwards, he will read on the doorways into old square courtyards the names of the old German families that once ruled the country, and he will come to an old church with great trees so bent with age that they stretch across the road and seem to try to sweep the opposite pavement. Turning then down a narrow lane, going through an archway, crossing a yard and going through yet another arch, he will come out upon the battlements and have before him the finest view to be obtained in any of the Baltic capitals. He will be looking down a sheer precipice on the ancient walls of the lower town, with the round grey towers that rise above them and the tall dark spire of the church of St Nicholas of the sailors, and far over the roofs of the town he will see the harbour with the ships coming and going about their business, while before him lies the great stretch of the blue bay, steamers lying in the roads, white-sailed yachts, sedate schooners slipping away northward to Finland far beyond the little island of Wulf, or moving westward between Nargon and the mainland, where again is open sea and clear horizon . . . I cannot believe that any man who has looked out to sea from Reval castle rock can ever be wholly happy unless he has a boat.

My imaginary wandering freemason of the sea, warmed by the thought that he has a share in all this, that he too can sail past those distant promontories, since his little ship is awaiting him in harbour, will then go down from the battlements by the rock path until the sea is hidden from him, but only for a moment. He will cross the railway lines and come out on the stony foreshore, where he will find a little square harbour for the shallow-draught fishing-boats and a row of wooden-trestle piers where those who have looked from the rock and have no boats try in vain to salve their pain

by hiring boats from other men. Here, too, he can listen with
amusement to the buying and selling of every sort of small
craft, which goes on with all the cheerful mendacity of
a horse-fair. This is the last refuge of boats discarded from the
Yacht Clubs, and here all kinds of ancient ruins are given
a coat of paint and bought by the unwary and sold by the
cunning, who know that those who have looked from the
battlements above them must have a boat or die. On the
foreshore men are always at work repairing little ships, and
you may find there illustrations for a whole history of Baltic
boat-building. Only a year ago I saw here one of the early
fishing-boats that were brought from the upper reaches of
the Volga, a flat-bottomed boat with planks sewn together
with strips of leather. In old days these boats used to be
brought to Reval by fishermen from Ostashkovo, in the
interior of Russia, who came for the summer fishing season,
sold their fish and their boats here, and bought little Esthonian
horses with which they returned by sledge overland in the
winter, to build new boats and come again next summer.[1]

But if castle rock and stretching bay and intimate
disreputable foreshore are among the glories and delights of
Reval, they are not the town itself, which, clustered about the
foot of the rock, has, of all the Baltic capitals, least of the
vices of a town and most of the virtues of a village. Nobody
in Reval tries to dress well, with the exception of a few young
women, and they, by the manner of their failure, do but
emphasize this cardinal virtue of their native place. Top-hats
were unknown there until the British Consul and Vice-Consul
spread awe and astonishment by wearing them on state
occasions, thereby startling the Ministers into ordering at least
two from England, for the use of the Cabinet. Not that for a
moment I would be thought to laugh at men who had the
courage to carry through a foreign policy against the almost
open threats of greater Powers, and have had the satisfaction
of seeing half Europe follow at their heels. I do but lament the

[1] Not far from here, in a river farther along the coast, I have seen a quite new dug-out, like
the boats of primitive man, hollowed with the axe out of a single tree. On a Russian river
I have been in a boat scarcely less simple, with an Evinrude motor fixed over the stern,
so near in Eastern Europe are the earliest and latest stages of civilisation.

introduction of those four top-hats and recognise that we, and
not the Esthonians, are to blame for them. Anyway, they are
very seldom to be seen, and I think that after that first
moment of horrified excitement everybody has come to
realize that Reval is not the place for them. In Reval nothing
is done for show, except, perhaps, an occasional march of
troops or fire brigade. And that you must have in any capital.
There is no single street in Reval given up to fine shops
and the parades of fools. Everything is decent, homely and
unflurried.

There are shops, of course, but the buying and selling in the
town is for the most part done in the older manner. The Reval
housewife does not go shopping for her day's provender. She
goes to market with a big string bag in summer and dragging
a little sledge at her heels in winter. In the middle of the town,
under the big Esthonian theatre, is a wide open space where
there is a food-market, and beside it little wooden booths
where you can buy string bags or even baskets to carry your
food in, doormats to wipe your feet on when you get home
(I bought one for the feet of *Racundra's* visitors), and
saucepans in which to cook it after you have arrived. The
market is made up of rows of tables on trestles, each with
a little roof. By old tradition, the sellers of each particular
kind of goods keep together. In this way they can keep a check
on each other's prices, and you, interested in quality, can
compare one cabbage with another or prod the breasts of half
a dozen chickens on different stalls before you make your
choice. In one part of the market you may walk between rows
of boxes full of pike, some of them still alive in bath-tubs, big
perch (two- and three-pounders are not the rarity that they are
at home) and baskets full of the little shining *killos*. In another
part of the market you are among green vegetables. In another
you buy hunks of meat wrapped in Esthonian newspapers
and dripping blood and printer's ink. At one side of the square
are the little carts which have brought all this food in from the
surrounding country. And there is a row of booths where, as
you pass, you hear the loud cheerful noise of people drinking
tea with great pleasure, with bits of sugar between their teeth,

and there are the farmers and their wives, sitting by the samovars on the trestle tables, eating enormous quantities of sausages. Besides this market there is another under the walls, for clothes and old iron, where I have picked up a block or a shackle now and again. This market is called "Lousy Market" by the inhabitants of Reval, and they ought to know. Both markets are in perfect keeping with the medieval character of the town.

*   *   *   *   *

Racundra lay five days in Reval, while her designer examined her all over inside and out to see what the builder had made of his dream, and set himself to put right as many as possible of our makeshifts. He made a new horse for the mainsheet to work on, gratings for the seats in the steering-well and battens for the sails, besides putting on the best of his old workmen to repair our damaged gaff. Meanwhile, we bought what we could of the things we needed, but finding that there were no blocks in Reval to fit our ropes, we decided to sail over to Finland and to finish our fitting out in Helsingfors. We rigged a yard for our squaresail, but found that the sail was too small to be of real use. The making and mending took time, and meanwhile the S.E. wind that would have carried us to Finland in a few hours was blowing itself out day after day.

We had plenty to do, of course, as one always has in even the smallest of ships. The gangway plank that we had rigged up over the stern was continually trodden by *Racundra's* visitors. We, too, had many friends to see in the town, and now and again went visiting in the dinghy in the harbour. *Baltabor* was there, having got in the morning of the day that we arrived, and Captain Whalley was to have lent me a Pelorus for the business of correcting *Racundra's* compass, but, clearing unexpectedly, as we had done in Riga, steamed away with the instrument on board. Then there was another English ship in the port, the *Maid of Erin*, a fine Bristol Channel pilot vessel, ketch-rigged, which had taken a cargo of boots to Petrograd. Her owner was a true merchant-adventurer, who told us that his real business was the breeding and selling of polo ponies. Without wishing to hurt *Racundra*'s feelings, we envied a little the broad decks and roomy hold of the *Maid of Erin*. She was three times our tonnage, of course, black and piratical in appearance, but what a ship to make a home of! Her owner, on the other hand, had plenty of admiration for *Racundra*, so we parted with mutual good feelings, made still warmer on our side by a present from the *Maid of Erin*, whose owner hailed me as I was rowing back in the dinghy from getting my papers cleared for Finland, and handed down a cake of plug tobacco, worth to me then many times its weight in gold. The Ancient and I shared it between us, and often, as we smoked, spoke of "that fine black pirate ketch" and wondered if we should meet her again. She was gone when we returned from Finland.

GROHARA ISLAND AND LIGHTHOUSE.

GROHARA ISLAND AND LIGHTHOUSE TODAY.

REVAL TO HELSINGFORS

ON August 30th, when we had our new gaff jaws and had put the battens into the sails, we were impatient to be off. The Cook remained in Reval, making room for my friend Mr. Wirgo, who at one time represented Esthonia in London and had arranged to make the passage with me to Finland. In early youth he spent some time in a sailing ship, and now owns the *Condor*, a little Swedish yacht, delightful in sheltered waters, but not fit for the crossing to Helsingfors. We had sailed round the harbour in *Condor* the preceding night, when Wirgo managed to tumble into the water while getting into a dinghy. The unfortunate effect of this was that when we had already started for Finland he complained of feeling ill, and after being dosed with aspirin from *Racundra's* medicine chest, had to spend most of the passage in his bunk. At the start, however, he was most impatient to be off, and was anxious that we should use the engine, which, however, was determined not to be used. He explained that, whatever happened, he must be back the day after tomorrow in order to take his wife to a ball in honour of the British Fleet, a squadron of which was expected. In his hurry, he actually towed us out of the harbour in the dinghy. That was at seven o'clock in the evening, and when he came on board again after a magnificent piece of work, for *Racundra* is a heavy little ship, the illness began which lasted until we were already within sight of the Finnish coast.

We started in the evening in the hope of getting a land breeze through the night, and this we did, though the breeze was so slight that when morning broke we were still close to the island of Wulf, which protects the Bay of Reval from the north. I steered all night until the dawn, which found us clear of the bay. It was pleasant work with the admirable leading lights of

Reval as a guide, and I took a number of bearings which confirmed the deductions made already about the gigantic character of our compass deviation. By half-past six we had passed Nargon and Wulf, and at eight we could see Wrangel island, east by north, and on the horizon the Revalstein three-masted lightship a little north of N.W. The wind dropped to nothing. It had only needed the dotting of an *i* and the crossing of a *t* to make it nothing before. We were simply drifting.

And then, quite suddenly, came the fog, and with it the slightest possible breath from the north, veering now and again. We steered, or rather pointed, for the ship could hardly be considered as under sail, N.E., E. by N., and E.N.E. The fog was a white, cool fog, and hid everything but the water within a few yards of the ship. The Ancient Mariner brought up the foghorn, and at the proper intervals we made the noises prescribed by law. Wirgo came up, looked about him, wondered rather dismally what his wife would say to him if she had to go to the ball alone, and retired to his bunk. The Ancient and I drowsed at the wheel in turns. There was something uncanny in being unable to see in a fog so white, so luminous in itself. Yet there it was, sure enough fog, as Huckleberry Finn would say, and we began to be worried by noises. Once or twice there were good recognizable noises made by other vessels: to these we cheerfully replied, proud of the fact that we could do as much ourselves. The worrying noises were the regular ones, signals from lighthouses, lightships and similar things, which we ought to have been able to identify and could not. The fog lasted until four in the afternoon. For some time before that the wind had been easterly, such as it was, and we had been pointing north. We had heard one particular noise which had disturbed us very much indeed. Hoots on a fog-horn and then the clear ringing of a bell, repeated accurately at three-minute intervals. Now, when a ship moves at all, the desires of those on board tend to make them believe that she is moving faster than she is in fact. Although, until we heard these signals, somewhere to the south of us and seemingly quite near, we had supposed *Racundra* was about half-way across the Finnish Gulf, yet when we heard them, it never for a moment occurred to us that they could be anything but signals from some lighthouse or lightship standing far out from the Finnish coast. We accordingly searched the *Baltic Pilot*, and examined the Finnish coast in both English and German charts, trying to find a place alleged to make such noises during fog. We could find nothing of the kind, and were actually beginning to be afraid that we had already come too near the land, when the fog rolled southward as swiftly as it had come, disclosing a horizon absolutely naked to the north and bare to the south except for a three-masted ship without sails and with curious swellings about the masts: the Revalstein lightship, which we had thought to be quite twenty miles astern. It was not until long afterwards that, idly looking over the chart of the Esthonian coast, I realized that the three-minute bell we had heard when wrapped up in that blanket was from the Kokskar Lighthouse, a few miles east of Wulf.

With the lifting of the fog came a wind from the N.E. which allowed us to sail northwards, humbled as navigators but renewed in hope as human beings. We knew now where we were, and the wind was taking us, not quite in the direction in which we wished to go, but pretty nearly in that direction. The only thing remaining uncertain was the deviation of our compass, and even with regard to that, we had a good deal of definite knowledge in place of the complete ignorance with which we had started from Riga. Later on our confidence was increased by the sight of a three-masted schooner also sailing north. She had her sails full and was going at a great pace, rapidly overhauling us, but when she passed us it was obvious that she was making much more leeway than even the generous *Racundra* allowed herself. We were sure that she too was bound for Helsingfors, or at any rate for a sight of the Aransgrund light-vessel, which is the outermost mark to show the way in. When she was almost hull down beyond us she went about and came sliding back again, and we decided that she had tacked on getting a sight of the light-vessel, which we knew must be somewhere a little east of our course. In this way, navigating very much from hand to mouth, we took the schooner as our guide and stood on as she had done, until at the same moment the Ancient sighted land ahead and I saw the light-vessel about five miles distant on our starboard bow. We stood on till we thought we could fetch the vessel on the other tack and then went about, just as dusk was falling, when we received an extremely disconcerting shock.

"It's the Aransgrund light-vessel sure enough," I had said, inspiriting myself, and added, by way of giving the crew and passenger some confidence in my knowledge to replace that which they had lost owing to the unfortunate reappearance of the Revalstein: "She will show two red lights, one from each masthead." I had just got this information from the *Baltic Pilot*.

Dusk fell. We were all on deck, looking for those red lights. And then the vessel showed no red light of any kind, but a white light that vanished and reappeared, one of those called 'occulting' on the charts and in the light lists.

"It isn't the Aransgrund, after all," said the passenger, but the Ancient supported me out of *esprit de corps*, and I, for our very honour, held to it that it was, in spite of the visible fact that it showed a white light instead of two red ones. I plunged down below and looked it up once more in the *Baltic Pilot*. "Two red lights." I searched the German chart. Red. The English chart that I had bought in the spring. Red again. And then, just as a sort of last hope that was really no hope at all, I looked at the only other chart I had, which was a small sketch of the minefields attached to a little book of *Notices to Mariners* given to me by Captain Whalley of the *Baltabor*. This little sketch chart in general showed no details, but one detail that it did show fairly glowed before my eyes. "Aransgrund Lt. V. White occ." The lights had been changed. It was the Aransgrund light-vessel after all, and I returned on deck with the book in my hand, my authority as navigator triply reinforced by the printed word of the British Board of Trade. It was a proud moment, but I had no time to enjoy it, for with the dark which fell suddenly upon us came a great wind out of the east, and *Racundra*, who had moved all day upon an even keel, was suddenly getting as much as she wanted. We could not fetch the light-vessel with that tack, so we stood on beyond it, then went about again, and fairly surged towards that white occulting light, which had become as it were a personal possession.

I suppose it was near eleven o'clock when the question of the colour of Aransgrund's eye was finally settled. At midnight we were within a cable's length of it, rushing through the dark without sidelights, dependent, as usual, upon the riding light which I carried in the well. I had hoped to go into Helsingfors by daylight, for I did not know the channel, and, more important, not only did not know the way to the Nylands Yacht Club, but did not know where to look for it, having been told vaguely that it was on an island. There are several hundred islands about, and the Club is not marked in German, English or Finnish charts. I therefore decided to take a pilot, and, having no flares, waved the riding light. For a long time there was no reply, when, thinking that perhaps he took our riding light for the ordinary white light carried on the open fishing-boats, we hooted at him with the fog-horn. This may have been extremely incorrect, but it had an instantaneous result. Figures moved on the lightvessel's decks. We heard shouts, and presently someone began swinging a lantern round in circles. They had understood, and all we had to do was to keep *Racundra* near the light-vessel while they launched a boat and put the pilot on board. This was not so easy as it might seem. Remembering the experience of Baltic Port, we had feared to take sail off her in spite of the wind, and, hove to, she was knocked about considerably, and drifted too near the vessel or else slipped off into the outer darkness. All this was probably due to our lack of knowledge of her. On later occasions I had her hove to under full canvas in the most decorous and ladylike manner. Anyhow, there was one horrid moment when we thought we were coming into violent contact with the light-vessel, the great bulk of which was heaving up and down in a most portentous manner right above us. The business of getting their boat out seemed very long, and we learnt afterwards that the pilot had been in his bunk and had to get up and dress.

"Who are you?" they shouted at us.

"English yacht," we yelled back, and after that, perhaps because the Fleet was expected next day and might avenge us, they did at last seem to get busy. There was the splash of a boat in the water, a bobbing lantern appearing and disappearing in

NYLANDS YACHT CLUB, HELINGFORS.

NYLANDS YACHT CLUB, HELINGFORS TODAY.

the waves, a bump, and a large Finnish pilot tumbled on board with: "Where do you want to go?. . Nylands Club? . . Right. Keep Grohara light so. Now, Captain . ." And with that, as pilots do, he expressed hunger and thirst.

I fed him and poured Riga vodka into him, while he asked me, "Did we not see you just as night fell, close by a three-masted schooner?"

"You did."

He laughed. "Do you know, we reported you by wireless to Helsingfors as a likely smuggler and told them to look out for you! Yours was the very last boat we thought would need a pilot."

I suspect that the reason why they had been so long in answering our signals from the lightship was that they supposed that, being smugglers, we were playing some new trick on them. The Esthonian smugglers, of whom there are many, make it their sport to tease the Finnish coastguards. I had heard much about it on the other side of the Gulf, where the smugglers are, as in old times in England, the heroes of the longshore population. One man in particular makes it his boast that he gets his cargo into Finland by a different method every time, and each time takes care to let the coastguards know the way they have been tricked. On one occasion he arrived at evening with a cargo of spirits covered with a thin layer of potatoes, and the Finns sealed up the hold of his vessel for examination in the morning. During the night he broke the seals, took out the spirit and disposed of it, and then woke the Customs officers while it was still dark and in a great state of perturbation asked them what he was to do, as in clearing up the deck he had accidentally broken their seals. "Fined two hundred marks for breaking the official seals." He paid the fine. Then, when he left, he sent a small keg of spirits to the Customs officers, with a note expressing his gratitude for having been allowed for so small a sum to bring in such and such a quantity of spirit. After many such exploits he was actually caught and imprisoned, and it was announced in the newspaper that he had been captured with fifteen hundred litres of spirit. He wrote indignantly to the editor to say that he had been captured with three thousand litres of spirit, not fifteen hundred, and wanted to know what had become of the rest. The Censor, he complained, did not allow his letter to be published.

When the pilot had finished his meat and drink we went on deck again, where Wirgo, recovered from his illness, was steering. I had left the matches on the cabin table and went down again to get them. Responsibility gone, the pilot in charge, and *Racundra* already safely across, I thought I would lie down for a moment. Out of the last thirty-two hours I had been twenty-eight in the steering-well. I lay down, just as I was, the box of matches in my hand; and three hours later, matches still in hand, rushed on deck in a panic, to find lights all about us, smooth water, the Ancient forward ranging the anchor chain, *Racundra* already brought to the wind and losing way, and the pilot on the point of saying "Let go". The chain rattled out. The pilot went below with me to drink more vodka and collect his fee. I paid the money and uncorked bottles half-asleep and wholly angry. Twenty-eight hours of steering in calm and fog, and then to sleep like a log during this last three hours of good sailing weather, just when I had meant to use the pilot in order to learn for myself how not to need him again!

HELSINGFORS: SWINGING THE SHIP

NEXT morning I came on deck to find *Racundra* in the delightful anchorage of the Nylands Yacht Club. The Club House is itself on an island, and with other islands of pink and

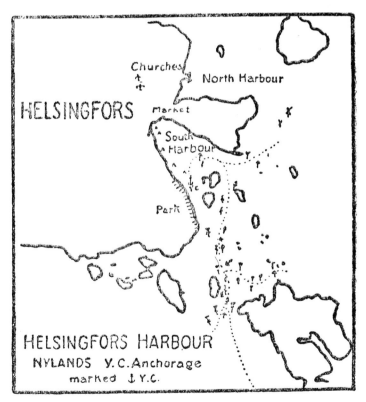

grey rock and a cliff on the mainland close above the water, gives perfect shelter to the little fleet that lie to mooring-buoys in this southern corner of Helsingfors harbour. The harbour proper lay before us, with white steamships along the quays, on which were the low Customs houses, the booths of a busy market, blue trams slipping swiftly by – a lively, comfortable scene – while over all were the great domed church and the cathedral spires that I have often admired from the sea when in ships bigger but not better than *Racundra*. Wirgo and I went ashore in the dinghy, he to hurry back to Reval by steamship and I to look for the friends who, after waiting for us last night in the Club House, had supposed that the fog had kept us on the other side of the Gulf.

In comparison with Riga and Reval, Helsingfors seemed not to have suffered from the war. The shops were full of all the things which for the last few years most Baltic towns have had to do without. With its clean white steamers and blue trams, it seemed more Swedish than Finnish. Finland, real Finland, is to be found in the country, not in the capital; and walking through the streets of this modern Western town, with its restaurants and taxi-cabs, I kept thinking of the simple country life I had tasted in Finland years ago. Near Hittola, by Lake Ladoga, paddling with a friend in a canoe-shaped boat, I remember finding a little ancient steam-yacht lying covered in on the reedy bank of a river. I was told that in its day it had made a voyage to Edinburgh and back. It was dropping into decay, that aged little steamer; those who had sailed in it were dead; the elk snuffed round it in the winter snow and wandered north to tell the reindeer, who perhaps, on the shores of the Arctic, had seen similar strange things. Looking north from that place to the Pole was nothing but wild country, lake, marshes, ragged forest and ice-infested seas. The little steam-yacht did not seem more foreign to it than this trim stone-built capital.

So far as *Racundra* was concerned, I wasted all that day in friendship. But early next morning there was a coughing and spluttering and spitting alongside, and I tumbled out to find that by that friendship *Racundra* was to profit after all. Commander Boyce had brought his little motor-boat, *Zingla*, to take me for a run round the harbour to show me the way through the buoys and out into the fairway, which I had missed by falling asleep as we were coming in. We ran out one way and ran in another through well-marked channels between the uncompromising rocks. The Finnish coast is not a coast on which to make mistakes, and I was glad I had not attempted the foolishness of trying to find the Club for the first time in the dark. Once you know where it is, however, it is easy enough. There are short cuts for small boats, but any yacht coming in here for the first time can do so safely by following the sailing directions for big ships until she is well into the southern harbour. Once there, she has but to follow the quay round into the southern corner of that harbour and, if she cannot find a spare buoy, drop anchor until morning.

After introducing me to a score or so of spar-buoys, eloquent in the language of up-turned and down-turned brooms, Boyce brought the *Zingla* back to *Racundra*, and the Ancient, for the first time – indeed, for the only time on the whole cruise, except for getting water – made up his mind to come ashore. He wanted a special size of sailmaker's needles, besides some scrubbing brushes and mops which he did not trust me to buy. He was not in the least interested in the town. "Towns," said he, "are all one and all dirt." This was a manifest libel on the spotless Helsingfors, but the Ancient had been a little embittered by the thick fringe of black grease which our waterline had acquired while lying in the harbour of Reval.

We spent an exciting and expensive morning. We bought new brass rowlocks for the dinghy which the builder had disfigured with coarse, badly galvanized iron rubbish which chafed the oars and did not fit. We bought rope fenders. We bought every block we could find that would fit our ropes, and regretted that we had not tried to buy them the day before, for we could only find half a dozen and could not wait while the shops sent to Äbö for more. We bought mops, woolly and stiff. We bought needles, shackles, hooks for the staysail, hooks for a hoisting strop for the dinghy, a vast hook with a strong spring clip for picking up a mooring-buoy, a tin of colza oil for the binnacles, brass clips for the main and mizen peak halyards, besides bread, butter, cheese, apples, Swedish oatcake, tobacco, stocking-caps, and a Finnish sheath-knife, a gorgeous piratical thing with a horse's head for a hilt, a handle inlaid with red and blue and yellow, and a curved sheath of black and scarlet leather. Finally, with full pockets and empty purses, both of us laden like pack animals, we staggered back to the quay, signalled to the Club boatman and were put on board our ship.

Then I went ashore again to inquire about a compass-adjuster, for I had seen a steamship being slowly shifted round and round a big wooden dolphin close astern of us. I had seen the white painted marks on the cliff and on buildings, so that I had no doubt as to what was being done. I was anxious to get our own compass corrected and a table of deviations drawn up, so that the homeward voyage might be made with a smaller proportion of guesswork. The Ancient, as always, was for starting at once.

"The compass is right enough," said he. "You found the way here with it and you'll find the way back."

I showed him the list I had made of observed inexactitudes, some of them as much as two and a half points (for the compass was immediately over the motor), but he was unconvinced, and I left him hauling up the sails, "to dry", as he said, but really, as I well knew, in hopes that, seeing them up, I should myself be persuaded that Helsingfors had done enough for us and that we might put to sea. When I came back from the harbour office he had already fixed the hook and strop on the fore-halyard and was prepared to haul the dinghy on board. He said nothing, but could not hide his disappointment when I told him that at eight o'clock next morning we were to be tied up to the dolphin and ready for the compass-adjuster who was to swing the ship.

I spent that evening in the Nylands Club. The Finnish six-metre boat, *Stella*, was there, back from racing at Cowes, and looking at her slim body, built for speed and nothing else, and then over the water to the stout, imperturbable *Racundra*, I thought how differently men take their pleasures on the sea. I would not have her as a gift, and I am sure that Mr. Donner, her owner, would turn in disgust from my comfortable cruiser. After dinner I went into the Club library and found there a really wonderful collection of sailing-books from all the countries of the world. I read over again that excellent little book by Thomas Fleming Day, the American; and then, for the first time, settled down to read McMullen. Few books on sailing fail to quote

McMullen, but his own book is rare, and I was glad enough to read, out here, on a Finnish island, the story of *Orion's* return from France and of McMullen's enviable death, sitting in the cockpit of *Perseus*, the tiller under his arm, in mid-channel on a star-lit night. I observed that McMullen, even in our temperate climate, laid up his ships early in September, and, looking at the calendar, remembered that we were far from home. It was after midnight before I put the book back on its shelf and, dropping over the pierhead into the dinghy, threaded my way in the dark through the little fleet to *Racundra's* gleaming portholes, for the Ancient, long asleep, had thoughtfully lit the cabin lamp.

I remember, in reading the logs of other people, experienced mariners, my disgust and annoyance when in a single sentence they dismissed the swinging of their ships. "Swung ship and drew up table of deviations." That is the professional manner of recording the event, and, if you are not such as they, you are left wondering how they did it. At least, that was so with me. I was left wondering and was ashamed to ask. But the business of ship-swinging is an interesting one, and whereas experienced mariners may skip the next few paragraphs, I am sure there must be inexperienced mariners, and even people who are not mariners at all, who will be glad to know how the thing is done and, in place of the cabalistic words "swung the ship", to have an actual picture of the ship being swung, or rather being lugged by main force round a wooden dolphin until she headed in turn on each one of the thirty-two points of the compass.

There was a hard N.E. wind blowing in the morning, and letting ourselves swing by a long line from the mooring-buoy to which we had made fast, we paid out line slowly as we worked stern first towards the dolphin, the anchor hanging deep in the water ready to hold us up. When near the dolphin, we loosed the buoy and held with the anchor while I got into the dinghy and took a warp across to the dolphin. Then we hauled up the anchor, and, shortening the warp, were swinging close by the dolphin while waiting for the arrival of the stout, red-faced, English-speaking Finn who spent every day of his life in the swinging of big ships.

The dolphin is a stout wooden erection, built of piles and so

"RACUNDRA" AT HELINGFORS (AFTER SWINGING THE SHIP).

HELINGFORS COMPASS SWINGING POST TODAY.

fixed in the bottom of the sea. Above water it is shaped like an inverted cone, on the top of which is a smaller cone with the narrower end uppermost. The lower cone, being bigger than the upper, forms a platform on which a man can walk. Round the upper cone is an iron belt working in a groove. At opposite sides of this belt are rings, and from these rings warps are taken to the bow and stern of the ship. The ship presses against the lower cone and, in whatever direction it may point, is kept in position by the warps to the revolving ring. A steamship is swung by simply steaming round the dolphin and in contact with it, stopping for a moment at each compass point.

The principle of the thing is simple enough. The dolphin may be taken as a fixed point. On the land, at a considerable distance from it, are marks so placed that when the ship is in contact with the dolphin and heading directly on one of these marks, it is heading towards a known point of the compass. By observing at this moment the compass to be corrected, it is easy to discover exactly what its error is on that particular point.

Just as we were making fast a small boat was rowed out to us carrying the red-faced Finn, who was a little disconcerted to find that the ship he was to swing was so very much smaller than the big vessels to which he was accustomed. However, he paid her a compliment or two when he heard where she had come from, and set very seriously about his business, after hurting our feelings a little by asking:

"Will I put my foot through if I stand on the cabin roof?"

"You will not," I replied.

"Ye can dance on her," said the Ancient, and with that the work began.

On the top of the cabin roof the Finn set up a heavy tripod carrying a sighting apparatus. At his command we pulled *Racundra* round that dolphin till he had one of the marks in line with his instrument. The dolphin was built for the swinging of big ships, and we had trouble in adjusting things so that we could use it for *Racundra*. The edge of the platform pressed against our shrouds and we had to take them down on one side. We decorated her side with all our fenders, and finding them insufficient, used our spare mattresses. However, in the end we

got the thing to work. The Finn would call out the actual
bearing, N., N. by W., or whatever it was, while I, darting to our
steering compass, called out the bearing indicated by the card
and the lubberline. We had in no way exaggerated the
inaccuracies. The Finn had brought with him two magnets
brightly painted, which he screwed down in the steering-well in
positions found by experiment. These magnets roughly
compensated for the effects of the mass of iron in the motor, so
that the compass became more or less correct. Then, point by
point, with the help of a couple of sailors borrowed from another
yacht, we pulled *Racundra* round and held her steady on each
one of the thirty-two points, noting at each point the difference
between actual and compass bearing. It took a long time, for the
wind was strong, *Racundra* heavy, and the Finn conscientious.
However, it was done at last, and down in the cabin, over a bottle
of vodka, the expert worked out his results, drawing up a table
on the Continental plan, while I translated them into a form
readier for actual use, in one column writing the course, and in
another the course to steer by our compass. By noon the work
was done. I put the Finn ashore and hung up the completed table
in the cabin.

With that we were both for starting while the wind held, late
in the day though it was. I took in water, made my farewells at
the Nylands Club, and, without anchoring again, cast off directly
from the dolphin and tacked out of the harbour.

HELSINGFORS TO REVAL

IT was 1.15 when we sailed, with the barometer at 30.1 and rising and the wind strong and easterly. The Nylands Club had been racing in the morning, and we met many of their boats coming in heavily reefed as we worked out through the buoyed channel which Boyce had shown me the day before. Three big grey ships of the British Fleet were at anchor in the outer harbour, but we were having our work cut out for us, twisting in and out among the buoys, and had small time to look at them. Outside there was a steepish sea, and we were getting a little splashed even before reaching Grohara Island, which we passed at 2.20.

Grohara is a small rock with a stout white lighthouse upon it, to be left to westwards. The last time I had passed it in daylight was in winter-time, when an ice-breaker was ploughing a way through the ice for a convoy of six vessels, and then there was the wreck of a little steamer that had tried to pass Grohara on the wrong side, and, for her error, was held there hard and fast on the rocks and was covered, hull, masts, and rigging, with a coating of thick ice so that she looked a ship of glass. The ropes by which the crew had lowered their boat were still hanging from the davits, swinging stiffly in the wind like glass pendulums. It was difficult to believe that the jolly little island at which we were looking today had been, only seven months before, the centre of that desolate scene. Now, instead of being a hummock in a snow-covered icefield, it was set in blue sea, splashed with white, the colours of the Finnish flag, while far to north of it we could see the little islands and rose-coloured rocks, and farther yet, on the pale skyline, the domes and spires of Helsingfors, a picture only less beautiful in its way than the romantic entrance to Stockholm.

From Grohara we steered S. and $\frac{1}{2}$ W., allowing rather more for drift than we should have done, and when we sighted the Aransgrund light-vessel, found it well away on the starboard bow. We steered to pass it close to, which we did at 4.7 (fifteen miles out from Helsingfors). By this time the swell was such that, though we were so near that on the top of a wave we could see the caps of the men on the light-vessel's decks, in the trough we could not see the vessel at all, not even the tops of her masts. The wind had been blowing hard easterly for most of the time we had been in Helsingfors, which was enough to account for the size of the waves. We shipped a little water, and the Ancient, obstinate as usual, put on his oilskins too late, and remarked sadly, "I am already wet in mine starn." I had put my oilskins on earlier, and had much amused him by carrying away on "mine starn" the blanket from my bunk as I rose from pulling the trousers down over the boots. Nothing will tame the prehensile tendencies of tarpaulins.

The wind had shifted a little, but our course gave us a point or two to spare, and we gladly took up the centreboard. Then in a hardish gust a faulty fastening in the mizen peak halyards came adrift and the peak fell down. We lowered the sail and tied it, lashing the boom to the rigging to prevent its banging about, and found that sailing as we were, not absolutely close-hauled, she steered perfectly without the mizen. We sailed her so the whole way across the Gulf, the wind being so lusty that we willingly accepted from its own strength this shortening of sail that we should perhaps have been too proud (or too lazy) to reef in for ourselves.

After this, which happened close by Aransgrund, *Racundra* settled down to her work and gave us a most exhilarating sail. It was a glorious day, bright hard sunshine, with cold in the air, as we get it in the Baltic at the back end of the year, a good wind heeling her over to the railing, stiff as she is, and that mighty swell lifting us sky-high and dropping us again into a blue depth walled by water. It was easy work steering, now that the mizen was gone, and we took it in long spells without the least fatigue. "This is better than coming across," said the Ancient Mariner. "Wind's all right, but it's fog as I can't stand. There's nothing worse for sailormen than when that fog he spreads himself on the water and we go howling around all blind."

At 6.25 the Ancient saw land on the port bow which we knew must be Kokskar and Wrangel Island, and almost at the same moment I got a sight of the Revalstein lightship to starboard. By nine o'clock we were between Wulf Island and Nargon, and could consider that we had crossed the Gulf. But we were very far from getting into harbour. The wind had been falling away towards evening and shifting to the south, and it took us as long to make the ten miles remaining as it had taken us to cover the thirty-five that we had left astern. Yet at this moment, before the sky wholly darkened, we could actually see the spires and chimneys of Reval, and the huge crane to the west of the town, looking like a gigantic bird with outstretched wings.

Then came complete darkness and a very cold night. We took turns at the wheel, the watch below occupying itself with the sidelights. I may say at once that the watch below envied the watch on deck, and, cold as it was, preferred the tiller to the sidelights. Fine copper sidelights they were too, pre-war, bought last year and horribly expensive. I had hesitated over their really shocking cost, but had remembered, "The smaller the ship, the more her need for good lights," had gone without new shoes, refrained from buying a new hat, and plumped for the best and most expensive sidelights I could buy.

All winter they had lain in my room beside compass and lead-line, log, sea-anchor, sextant and cabin-lamp, and, shining there with the promise of the summer's cruise, had warmed me with an inward glow, what time the snow

PORT OF REVAL.

PORT OF REVAL TODAY.

was deep in the garden outside and the thermometer stood resolutely at zero or considerably below. On the smooth passages from Riga to Runö and from Runö to Paternoster they had burned well enough; and it had been a pleasure, steering through the quiet night, to know that the green eye and the red were gleaming brightly for any other ship to see. But during the gale that followed they had failed us. We had done our hopeless beating under jib and mizen, trying to make Baltic Port, with our lights out. We had wallowed about in the night between Pakerort and Nargon knowing that we showed no light to any other ship. Again, going into Helsingfors, as the wind got up off Aransgrund, they had failed us, and by now it was abundantly clear that they were but fair weather friends and would burn only in a comparative calm.

To-night the watch below cleaned them, trimmed them, filled them, brought them on deck and set them in their places only to see them go out abruptly and decisively as soon as they were there. He took them below, trimmed them again, wrapped them in sackcloth for shame and as protection, and brought them out again, cuddled close as if they had been favourite lambs and he a careful shepherd, only to see them drop into darkness the moment they felt the wind above the cockpit coaming. He devised a new method of protecting them, thought of some other way of keeping them alight, took them below, retrimmed, relit and brought them up again, nursed like babies, to receive another blow from Fate upon the optimism that grew less sturdy as the night wore on. Then the man at the wheel, of course, thought that he could do better, so we changed jobs for half an hour until the other man's optimism was hammered into the same shrinking, tender state as that of the first. Finally we both gave it up and kept them muffled in the galley, hoping to be able at least to show one dying flash of the right colour to any ship that we might meet. The riding light, a simple, cheap, ordinary affair, burned well, and we kept it among our feet in the cockpit, for warmth and to be able to flourish it in case of urgent need.

We had to beat the whole way into Reval, and beating is not the thing that we are best at. We could, however, get along with short legs to eastward and then long legs in more or less the right direction. There was no difficulty about it. Reval is a good place to make in the dark. Just east of the harbour mouth are two lights, one standing well back and very high and another almost on the foreshore and low. These two, kept one above the other, lead the whole way in until one can see the lights of the harbour entrance. Moreover, one of them fades and goes out the moment the approaching or departing mariner has strayed to east or west of the safe channel. So we stood close-hauled as near southerly as we could until the light went out, then went about and sailed on the other tack while it shone out again, came under the high light, slipped clear of it and again faded and went out, whereupon we tacked once more. This we repeated continually, creeping slowly nearer all the time, growing colder and colder as the night wore on. Towards morning a little steamer passed us and anchored far ahead, close by the harbour. Soon after that we could see the electric lights on the quays, a light or two up in the sleeping town, and the riding lights of the men-of-war in the western corner of the bay. We had long lost the muffled moon, and began to rejoice in our slow speed, which promised to bring us, as indeed it did, among the crowd of anchored schooners and other small vessels in the roads just as the sky was lightening in the east.

Dimly ahead of us we could see the pale hulls of ships, and already over to the east the dark sky seemed to blench. And then, as it were quite suddenly, there was more light, and we saw, as if at a signal, the sails of a schooner coming out of harbour, followed by another and another of the ships that had been waiting for the dawn. We passed the little steamer lying at anchor, tacked through the ships in the roads, crossing and recrossing the paths of the outgoing schooners, and came to the harbour mouth when in the blue mist of early morning the red and green lights on either side of the entrance glittered more like butterflies than lamps.

They went out just as we turned in, took off our staysail and rounded up to one of the buoys off the Yacht Club mole. We tied the damp sails till we could dry them in the sun, and while the Ancient cleared up on deck, I went below and, with fingers so cold that I could hardly strike a match, lit the Primus and boiled water. With that we drank the last of our English rum, and now, suddenly, too tired to talk, dropped each on his bunk and slept.

IN BALTIC PORT.

BALTIC PORT TODAY.

REVAL TO BALTIC PORT

SEPTEMBER 5th, 6.20 a.m. Barometer 30.25. We wasted a day in getting provisions and taking on board the fine new gratings for the seats of the steering-well and the new iron horse for the mainsheet, which we stowed in the forecastle for use next year, as its mass of iron would have played all sorts of tricks with our newly adjusted compass. The wind that would have served us so well, had we been able to start before, had died away, and was replaced early this morning by a slight breath from the S.E., with which we drifted out of harbour on a clear morning while the smoke of the Reval chimneys was of divided opinions as to what wind was blowing or whether any wind was blowing at all. We, however, had made up our minds that the wind was S.E., and set the balloon jib as a spinnaker, and were happy to find that it agreed with us and drew. By nine o'clock we had brought Karlo Island due W. An hour later we had cleared it and were steering to pass close by Surop, the balloon now set as a staysail.

Changes of sails were always a delight to the Ancient Mariner who, tenderly handling our little tablecloths and pocket-handkerchiefs, remembered sail-shifting in the famous ships of long ago.

"My best sailing," he would say, looking critically at our balloon, "was in the *Demooply* (*Thermopylae*). There was she and the *Kutuzak* (*Cutty Sark*), and I was in the *Demooply*. In those days there was racing between those ships, and not a man in any ship but would have his bet on one or other, if it was only a pound of tobacco. Double crews they had, and when I first sailed with the *Demooply* I thought officers and men were all mad. We never left those ships alone. We were shifting one sail or another sail for every little change of wind. Double crews, but none too many for the work, and before I had been on board a week, I was as mad as all the rest. There was real sailing done in those days."

To-day, however, no ingenuities in setting canvas would have been of any use to us. There ensued a period of absolute calm, accompanied by a psychological storm, for the Cook demanded that the motor should be used. The Ancient and I have never been shipmates with a motor before, and we do not like them, trust them or understand them. After long opposition, and trying to prove that we were really moving, although the water was like glass, we did at last try to wind it up, and found that it would not go; whereupon the Cook asked that it should be thrown overboard, and was not pacified on being told that it was valuable as ballast. However, when a breath of wind came diffidently down to us from the N. and we got steerage way again, she relented and gave us luncheon on deck. At 3.30 we had Surop Lighthouse abeam, and saw a flight of twenty-one duck just off the point. At four we passed the new Surop blinking-buoy, and saw the four-masted German schooner which had followed us out of Reval, away to N. of us by Nargon, with all staysails and spanker set, a fine sight, but too far away for the camera. By six o'clock we were just moving through the water N. of Fall, and it was already clear that the spell which lies on me when going westward along this strip of coast was not to be broken.

Every time I have sailed from Reval to Lahepe Bay or to Baltic Port, I have been becalmed off Surop and spent the night drifting between there and Pakerort. I have spent as many as thirty hours on this passage of a score of sea-miles, and I face it always with desperate resignation. This was to be my record quick passage. *Racundra* easily beat both *Slug* and *Kittiwake*, for she, first of my ships, covered those magic score of miles in under the twenty-four hours. The spell is not laid on that passage going the other way, but you will remember that it was precisely between Pakerort and Surop that we had to spend that wild night after our futile attempt to beat into Baltic Port with a broken wing.

This night was to be the completest contrast to that night of storm. In scarcely rippled water, across broad patches smooth as oil, we crept slowly towards Pakerort. There was a fiery sunset over the sea to the N.W., against which the sails of the little fishing-boats on the bank off the promontory were as if picked out with a fine brush and Indian ink. We saw, through the binoculars, the little fleet scatter as the twilight fell. Some made off beyond the point, and three, under sails and oars, slipped homewards into Lahepe Bay on the nearer side of Pakerort. Black silhouettes against that fiery sky, they turned suddenly into pale blots moving against the darker mass of the cliff. And then the cliff itself faded, and the lighthouse above it shone out, and there were stars and a wind that you could feel on the back of your hand, but would not blow a match-flame crooked. The Cook, extremely angry with the motor, and with us for our philosophic, indeed almost relieved, acceptance of the fact that the smelly little creature would not work, went to bed. The Ancient and I smoked together in the steering-well, after lighting our sidelights, which on this calm bright night burned magnificently. We rounded Pakerort and then were met by a very slight breath from the S.E., against which we beat slowly into Roogowik.

At anchor, off the harbour, was a ship of the Esthonian Navy. Signal lights were chattering between her and the harbour. Small boats with lanterns passed to and fro. The faint wind brought us the noise of music on board. And then, as we came nearer, someone on board must have noticed us, and we were presently drenched with the blinding cold glare of a searchlight. "They think we're another little ship-of-war," said the Ancient, "and they're afraid we're going to ram them." If not, it was with very bad manners that they kept us in such a glare that we could hardly see what we were doing and could not see the tiny light of Baltic Port. At last, however, they tired of this, and when we had recovered our eyesight, we found the little red light of the harbour, stood on the port tack till it had turned to green, and then, keeping it so, tacked towards it and, at 1.30 a.m., rounded into the harbour.

We found not the comfortable harbour I had known before, but one of, temporarily, half that size. Two big schooners were lying berthed side by side against the outer mole, and we had to tie up to the new tarred quay which walled off the anchorage, now dry land, where, with other happy little boats, *Kittiwake* had her moorings last year. We were glad of the new fenders from Helsingfors, and, getting ourselves pretty black, managed to keep *Racundra* clean. We tied up fore and aft, had a tot of hot but inferior rum, and went to bed.

OLD BALTIC PORT AND NEW

I first found Baltic Port in *Kittiwake*, and having found it, made it our headquarters for a happy summer of minor exploration. I had heard of it as the Russian Naval Port, and imagined it a kind of Sheerness, busy with motor-launches, steam pinnaces and other forms of naval activity. I found it a sleepy little old-time harbour, made by moles from the shore enclosing a square basin, the shore being left as it always had been, so that the fishing-boats used to beach themselves upon it at full speed, a man jumping on the thwart and swinging backward from the shrouds to save the mast at the moment of grounding, when they often ran a boat half out of the water. The day *Kittiwake* struggled in, there was a British steamship, a Wilson boat, the *Cato*, in the harbour, and though she is a small ship, she left very little room for anything else. I think the *Cato* called twice that summer, but all the rest of the traffic there was made up of local schooners, and the harbour-master had little else to do but to sail a smart little skiff to the bank off Pakerort for fishing, or across to Roogö, or round between the islands to see how fast she could do it. There was never any hurry in Baltic Port, and there seemed to be a lot of holidays. On one of them I watched the crew of the *Cato* beaten at football by a local team. Eleven played on each side, but the *Cato's* crew had no spare men, whereas every man in the Port was waiting round the field to take his turn in the local team, and as one tired another took his place. On another the *Cato* lowered away a lifeboat, and we went off to the fishing grounds under a dipping lug. At one side of the harbour was a low stage beside which a grey Government launch was moored, end to end with a converted fishing-boat, partly tarred and partly painted blue, in

which, on Sundays, stray visitors were transported to
the Roogö islands and back. Once a week the three or four lads
on the Government launch took her out to sea on mysterious
business. But for the most part they lay half naked on the stones
on the far side of the mole or had splashing matches with
each other.

The little town had much the same character. Small boys
played *gorodki* (a very exciting Russian form of skittles) on the
broad streets that were nearly all grass. Cattle grazed there. I met
three sheep coming out of church with the sedate manner of
respectable parishioners. I watched a hare playing by the railway
station, where a large part of the population used to meet in the
evenings to see the train come in from Reval. There was a post
office, and I think three or perhaps even four shops. There was
also a fire brigade, who played various instruments and now and
again stirred the whole town by giving a concert. Some young
women visitors tried to organize a flag-day there, but it was
a failure, though everybody in the town was very much
interested and asked them how much they got. There could not
be a pleasanter little place.

But with growing traffic in the Baltic, such quiet could hardly
continue in a port which in all but the most exceptional winters
is free from ice. There are fifteen fathoms of water between the
mainland and Roogö, and the water is deep almost to the shores.
Long after the way into Reval is blocked with ice, ships can
come freely into Roogowik and into Baltic Port itself. Peter the
Great and Catherine after him realized what could be done with
such natural advantages, and relics of their work show what
Baltic Port may yet become. Just north of the harbour is the old
fort, carved out of the cliff itself, with deep moats which must
once have been sunk to sea-level, or very near it. There are the
old bastions, cunningly laid out as in Peter's project, the old gun-
positions, with sheer cliff below them on the side facing the bay,
and on all other sides cliffs also, invisible from a yard or two
away, made by cutting the moat down from the high land – a
moat a hundred yards across, winding this way and that all
round the fort, with perpendicular sides of solid rock. The work
was done with convict labour and the labour of prisoners of war,

and all this stuff cut out of the rock was tipped into the sea to make the mole that he had planned to stretch across the bay and to turn it into the finest enclosed harbour in the Baltic. I have seen old pictures of the work in progress, the masons busy in boats about their business. Yard by yard the mole was pushed out to sea, and from Roogö Island over on the other side, where you can still see that the natural line of the coast is broken, they began building another fort and a second mole to meet the first. On that side they did not get so far, but on this the spar-buoy north-west of the harbour marks the end not of a natural reef but of Peter's artificial causeway and breakwater, which, unfinished as it is, serves to protect the stretch of beach always covered with fishing-boats and drying nets between the fort and the harbour. When I was there, there were wild roses growing in the fort. Columbines and Canterbury bells were growing in the moat, and, lying up there on the top of the old gun-positions, I used to spend hot afternoons looking out to sea, thinking of Peter and his passion for ships, and eating the wild strawberries.

On the shingle below the fort where the women sit with their children, fastening small flat stones as sinkers to the bottoms of the nets, I saw a German mine being put to a purpose precisely opposite to that for which it was intended. The fishermen were building a new boat. Her keel was laid and they were putting on the planking. They were busy steaming the planks, and their boiler was a German mine, emptied of its explosives and neatly fixed over a small furnace of stones from the beach. How they had managed to get the explosives out I do not know, but here was the mine with a good fire under it, boiling away like a domestic kettle, and being used for making boats instead of for their destruction.

My chief friends in Baltic Port in those days were the harbourmaster and his wife, who fed me with coffee that day when I first came in there, so tired that I fell asleep with my head on the table before ever I could put the coffee to my lips. With him I used to sail in his little skiff, which he could steer by merely shifting his own huge weight forward or aft. With her I used to remember my own North country, where also the good wives will tell you what a fool you be at the very moment when they are drying your boots and mixing you a hot grog to save you from the cold that you have earned. I met her one day going to Reval with great bundles of lilac blossom under her arm for a friend in town, and on her head, instead of the pretty green shawl she wore at home, a hat with an enormous white ostrich feather, exactly in the front of it, waving like a helmet plume. She had had this feather for nineteen years, she said, had never washed it, had never gone into Reval without it, and yet it was still as white as when it was new. It had survived many hats. Nineteen years before, her husband, a sailor then, came back from a voyage. She had forgotten where he had been, but no matter; he came back in a hard winter, when even Baltic Port was frozen in, and he left his ship stuck in the ice and came home to her to Pakerort Lighthouse on Christmas Eve, across the frozen seas, with two ostrich feathers, this and another, between his shirt and his skin, so escaping the Customs officers. "And were you pleased with him?" I asked, and was delighted by her reply. "Pleased with him?" said she. "Why, I gave him a proper talking to straight away for being such a fool as to bring two white ostrich feathers. If he'd had but a ha'porth of sense he'd have brought one white one and one black."

What with talks with the harbourmaster and his wife, whose roughness of tongue was only a defence for the softness of her kind heart, with the lighthouse-keeper from Odensholm, who used to sail in now and again in a little half-decked sloop, and with the skippers and crews of the little sailing vessels which, but for the *Cato*, made all the traffic of the harbour; what with days fishing on the river six miles away, whither I took *Kittiwake's* dinghy on a country cart, and days in wind and sunshine on Peter's fort and the cliff by Pakerort, I liked Baltic Port well at all times, but perhaps best of all in the evenings, after sundown, when we used to sit on *Kittiwake's* green cabin roof, there being no other dry place after the swilling of the decks. The old watchman would carefully lay his long pipe on the bench outside his wooden hut, and wander slowly round the harbour to climb the rickety iron ladder and light the light at the harbour mouth. When we were there, in May and June, it was never really dark. A guitar would tune up in one of the schooners, an accordion in another. Most of the little ships carried family parties, skipper, wife and little skipperlets, and there would be dancing on the decks, while the local beauties would lie back in the stern-sheets of the dinghy belonging to the Government launch and be rowed about by the sailors. And, just at this time, cutter or schooner would warp to the harbour mouth, and, with the glow of the evening sky on her sails, slip silently away to make the most of the land breeze that comes with the setting of the sun.

Now all is changed. There, where *Kittiwake* lay to her anchor, is now the new quay, on which they say there is to be a railway and a crane. Things may be better when the works in progress are finished, for new moles are to be built and the harbour will be twice the size. Things will be better for the big ships busy on the Russian trade, but I doubt if they will be better for us. The harbour-master is too busy to sail his little skiff. The few shops have already multiplied to a dozen or more, and whereas, in the old days, the harbourmaster's wife was only sometimes willing to give lodging to those whom she counted her friends, there is now a regular hotel, the rooms of which are full of busy, serious people, interested in the new activity of the port. Big steamers with steel cables will soon leave no room for the schooners, and little ships like *Racundra* and *Kittiwake* will never again find Baltic Port the delightful lazy anchorage that it was a year ago.

FISHING BOATS AT BALTIC PORT.

ONE OF THE ROOGÖ BOAT-HOUSES.

THE ROOGÖ ISLANDS

WE did not call at Roogö in *Racundra*, for we were
hurrying to get southwards to the places we had not yet
visited. But the year before, in *Kittiwake*, we had sailed round
between the two islands, and had landed at the jetty that you
can see from the quay at Baltic Port and walked all over Little
Roogö. The inhabitants of these islands, men, women and
even pigs, are patriotic Swedes. When I first rounded up there,
three aged men and a pig strolled out on the jetty to inspect
us, and began at once by asking me if I spoke Swedish. I told
them in Swedish that I did not, or only very little, but they
were persuaded that I was only teasing them, and when at last
they were convinced they lost all interest and strolled
disappointed away. The pig remained on guard, and when
I landed, resented my presence, worrying round me like
a good housedog. I am sure if I had been a Swede he would
have wagged his tail and licked my hand.

A day or two later, however, Leslie joined us from Reval,
and we crossed to the island again. He had lived in Christiania
and Copenhagen and was sure of being able to make himself
understood. A man on the jetty who had watched us sailing
over had disappeared by the time we arrived. I suppose he was
one of those whom I had disappointed by not being a Swede.
But Leslie went boldly up past the little windmill to the first
of the wooden cottages to buy eggs. He returned discomfited
with the news that this cottage was inhabited exclusively by
widows who did not keep hens. I had gone farther and found
another cottage, outside which some sort of Sunday
parliament was in progress, half a dozen men and two or three
women sitting on logs and stools, the men smoking long

pipes. Spurred by competition as a linguist with Leslie, I shouted out boldly, "Har ni naugra egg?" with electrical effect. A woman with a white shawl over her head leapt up and disappeared on the run towards some outhouses. The gathering broke up. Everyone slipped away and ostentatiously busied himself or herself with something or other, and when Leslie and the Cook came up they refused to believe that I had done anything but terrify the population. Gradually the men and women, having as it were put themselves in the right by being found busy, deserted their imaginary occupations and came half-heartedly towards us. In the background I could see the fleet runner in the white shawl and green petticoat darting from outhouse to outhouse with a basket. An old humpbacked witch, certainly not over four and a half feet high, with a bright maroon shirt hanging loose outside her petticoat, hobbled from a cottage to stare at us from afar, and presently the egg-gatherer, shielded by a group of friends, drifted towards the gate where we stood.

The same questions were asked that had been put to me on my first coming by the old men on the jetty. Were we Swedish? Where had we come from? How long had we been in Baltic Port? My Swedish, having obtained eggs, faded away behind Leslie's Scandinavian fluency. We bought butter, but had no paper to put it in. The old man who sold it us said at once that we could take their saucer and bring it back in the evening when we had done with it, a remarkable proof of the honesty of the islanders and their consequent belief in the honesty of others. In Russia such a loan would have been unthinkable. On the mainland here, the canny lender would have asked for a deposit of at least twice the value of the saucer. We settled the matter by putting the butter in the biggest of our tin mugs.

We walked out of this village of Storaby together with three mottled cows, driven by a woman with a handkerchief on her head of red, orange and white, a deep rich green skirt and a bodice of bright purple, flaming like a tulip. As we walked we were joined by other women and other cows, until at last there was a considerable herd, driven by four women with

long sticks over an open space of moorland, green grass and
swamp, with grey rocks showing through the turf. Fields on
either hand were enclosed with stone walls built without
mortar, like our walls in Lancashire and Westmoreland, but
lower, because the stones are round, sea-worn boulders and
harder to fit together than the flat slates at home. Presently we
broke away from our companions and made for the woods to
get out of the wind and find a place for dinner. The woods
were even wetter than the open country, carpeted with moss
that squelched under the feet. They were not the pinewoods of
the mainland, but birchwoods, and under their silver stems,
wherever the ground was not a morass, were lilies of the
valley. Near the far edge of the woods we stopped and cooked
our dinner under the shadow of a great rock on a good fire of
birch, which is the best of all trees for the heat that is in it.
Climbing to the top of the rock and standing upon it, I could
just see the glint of water, and beyond it the dark woods of the
other or Greater Roogö.

After dinner, a pipe and some flower-gathering, we went
slowly out of the woods and across one stone wall after
another until we came down on the western shore of the island
and found a scene of astonishing strange beauty. The shore,
flat, with scattered boulders, seemed to slip unwillingly into
the sea. The water, dotted with rocks, so that it looked as
if one could walk ankle-deep from one island to the other,
was quite smooth. And in the middle of this shining water,
a quarter of a mile away, was a green islet, with a little wood
at its southern end, and behind this wood, her bows and tilted
bowsprit showing and her tall masts heeling over above the
trees, was a black, two-masted sailing-ship, aground. Beyond
were the bluer waters of the bay, ruffled with wind; beyond
them again the wooded shore of the mainland. It might have
been the opening scene of a boy's story of a pirate island. Nor
did the scene lose any of its romantic character as we came
nearer and saw the black tarred ship reflected in shallow
water, through which the grass rose, disturbing her image,
while at her stern a ladder was set with its foot resting on the
green meadow. How she got there I could not say, nor how she

A ROOGÖ WINDMILL.

A POST WINDMILL TODAY.

proposed to depart thence. The waters of the Baltic deepen along these shores, when the wind is from the N. and W., but I did not think that they could rise so high as to float this vessel, which, undamaged, her anchor out as if in deep water, her masts and rigging intact and fretting the sky, seemed by the ladder, with a gesture of renunciation, to have given up the sea for good and made the land her resting-place for ever.

We walked on southwards along the shore, looking at the windmills, which are many and small, like large dovecots, to the village of Lillaby, which, though called the lesser, is really the larger of the two on the island. It is a fishing village, and on the shore close by are many little artificial harbours, each big enough for one or at most two small open boats. At the head of each of these little shallow landing-places is a shed, hung with the nets and other instruments. There were long nets on hoops, with wide wings opening from their mouths, for the catching of pike, and the usual very fine nets, like gossamer, some of them stained a faint blue, for catching the little silver *killos* which, salted or preserved in oil, are a staple of Esthonian diet. Then there were the buoys for the nets – wooden buoys, each one carved so that its owner would know it; buoys shaped like dumbbells, balls, crosses, with flags and without flags, lettered and unlettered.

The village itself is a group of little wooden cottages, painted for the most part yellow, with a few blue ones among them, each one set higgledy-piggledy in a little bit of ground with apple-trees, which just then were in full bloom. It seemed at first deserted, but as we turned up towards it from the edge of the sea we saw two old men leaning on a gate in conversation. Both of these men, and a younger man who joined them later, were dressed like sailors, in blue striped jerseys under their coats. Leslie, as Scandinavian scholar, was thrust forward as spokesman, and had a great success, fully making up for my first failure on the quay at Storaby. It seemed that news of our arrival had already crossed the island. They knew that we were English, and the elder of the two, evidently the philosopher of the place, told us that it was no wonder we could make ourselves understood, since Swedish, Danish, Norwegian, German and English were all from the same stem and were the five great languages of the world. Politely trying to make us feel at home and among friends, he asked how we were getting on with our coal strike and wanted us to tell him about Ireland, which he confounded with Courland, though when Leslie said that the Courlanders were now independent and called their country Latvia, he at once explained that he meant a country somewhere that belonged to England.

The inhabitants of Lillaby are very timorous of strangers. Besides the three fishermen, we could not get speech of a soul, though we saw several peeping at us through cottage windows as we passed on through a seemingly deserted village. We wanted water, and saw a girl in an orchard by a pump, so the Cook went in there to ask leave to draw some for herself, but the girl rose and fled silent into the cottage, and the Cook filled her can at the pump and came away. Afterwards we saw the girl's head, looking after us round the corner of the wall.

We did, however, have one other interview, but that was with a pig. We had come on the nearest thing to a street to be found on the island – low stone walls, with a mud lane between them, and barns and painted cottages on either side. I wanted to photograph it, but wanted something in the foreground, and since there were no inhabitants, and I remembered that rather hostile pig I had met on my first landing, said aloud, "If only there were a pig." At that moment we turned the corner of a barn, and there in the very middle of the lane lay a pig indeed. It was such a pig as that described in a novel of the Goncourts', which slept a sleep that could only be due to a heart of gold and a stomach of iron. It lay on the edge of a shadow, in the muddiest bit of road, its forepaws idly crossed, like the hands of a gentlewoman resting from her knitting. She (for it was a feminine pig) raised her head and grunted at us. The ice was broken. I approached her with affectionate words, camera in hand, begging her to move a yard, no more, into the sunshine. She understood me perfectly, moved into the sunshine, and took up one pose after another which she judged characteristic of her temperament. I asked her to snuffle in the mud and she snuffled in the mud. I took off my hat to the pig and thanked her, and she, after showing that she was not to be outdone by her owners in kindness to those who could talk Swedish to the inhabitants of Roogö (for I feel sure that if it had not been for Leslie's conversational successes she would have treated me in the manner of her brother of Storaby), returned sedately to her place, judged the lengthening shadows, chose the dampest spot that had recently been warmed by the sun, and resumed her calm and contemplative attitude of benevolent repose. Unfortunately every one of the photographs was a failure.

We met no one else on the island and came out from the village on wide open grassland, and over that to the woods, where we gathered lilies of the valley, made fire on a stone, and tea, which we drank squatting on our heels, which squelched beneath us in the marsh, while a woodpecker shrieked and jeered in the birch-trees overhead. Then, as evening fell, we hurried back to *Kittiwake*, made sail again, and returned to our anchorage in Baltic Port.

THE SHIP AND THE MAN

SAILING from Baltic Port, one of a crew of four in another man's ship, I came to the far end of the Dagorort Peninsula, and there had an experience which I cannot refrain from putting in this book, so full it was of the romance of those rarely visited waters.

*   *   *   *   *

We had anchored half a mile from the shore off the place that is called Ermuiste, which means "the terrible", for it is a place of many wrecks, a rocky point open to the widest sweep of the winds across the Baltic Sea. We had not dared to go nearer, and I was glad we had not, for, as I rowed ashore in the little boat, I passed many rocks awash and saw others a foot or two under water. There were dark purple clouds rising over the sea to the N.W., wind was coming, and we were impatient to be off again, to find shelter, or at least to put some miles of sea between us and that notorious coast. But there was still sunlight on the rocky shore and on the dark pinewoods that ran down almost to the water's edge and on the little wooden pierhead, unmarked on the chart, which, seen through binoculars, had tempted us to run in and look for information and supplies. Beyond the pierhead was a little stretch of beach where I meant to land. But, looking over my shoulder as I pulled in, bobbing over the waves in my little boat, I could see none of the things that a pierhead usually promises. There was no watchman's hut on the pier, no smoke above the trees, no cottages, no loafers, no fishermen, no sign of any kind of life. And then, coming nearer, I saw that the pier was in ruins. Much of its planking had gone, great beams were leaning perilously over from it, and here and there masses of it had actually fallen into the water. I wished to waste no time, and was on the point of turning and pulling back to the ship, when I saw something else more promising than the pier. Just within the forest that stretched down to the beach, almost hidden by the tall pines, was the great golden body of an unfinished ship. Where a ship was building, there, surely, must be men, and I rowed in confidently past the ruined pier, slipped off my shoes, rolled up my trousers and, jumping overboard, pulled the little boat through shallow water and up on a narrow strip of small pebbles.

Then, walking up into the shadow of the trees, I came to the ship, the upper part of which, far above my head, was glowing in the splashes of sunshine that came through the tops of the pines which brushed the sides of the ship as they waved in the gathering wind. There was not a man to be seen, or a hut for men, nor was there sound of hammers or any of the usual accompaniments of shipbuilding. But for the ruined pier and that golden hull in the shadows among those tall trees, the coast might have been that of an undiscovered island. And then I began to notice one or two things about the ship herself which seemed a little odd. She was a very large ship to be building on that bit of coast, where there is no real harbour and the most ambitious launches are those of the twenty-foot fishing-boats which a man builds during the winter to earn his living in the summer months. She seemed even larger than she was, as ships do on land, shut in there among the trees that pressed about her as if they had grown up round her. And her lines were not those of a new ship. There was something a little old-fashioned about them, as though she were an unfinished masterpiece of an older period. A few schooners of her type survive today among those "laibas" that carry timber and potatoes round the Esthonian coast, and they outsail those modern ships in which an obstreperous motor, tucked away in the stern, makes up for the want of the love and thought that went into the lines of the older vessels. And then I saw that I was wrong in thinking that she had been newly planked. The upper planking was new, certainly, ruddy gold where the sun caught it, but lower down her hull was

SHIPS THAT PASS....

weathered. Only the topmost planks had been freshly put on, and as the eye descended from them it passed imperceptibly from a new to an old piece of shipbuilding. The keel, laid on great stones, was joined to them by moss. There was lichen upon it, and on the foot of the stern-post was a large, bright cluster of scarlet toadstools.

Just then I found a narrow, lightly worn track running from the ship farther into the forest. I walked along it, and only a few score yards away, but quite invisible from the shore, I came out of the silence and the trees into a small clearing and a loud noise of grasshoppers. There was a tiny hayfield, not bigger than a small suburban garden, a cornfield, perhaps three times the size, and an old log cabin with a deep thatched roof, an outhouse or two, a dovecot and pigeons fluttering about it.

The pigeons fluttered and murmured, but no dog barked and no one answered when I knocked at the low door of the hut. I knocked again, and then, doubtfully, tried the wooden latch, opened it and walked in. A very little light came through the small windows, heavily overhung by the deep thatch. The hut was divided into two rooms. In the first were a couple of spinning-wheels, one very old, black with age, the other quite new, a precise copy of it, the two contrasting like the upper planking and the keel of that still unfinished ship. There was also a narrow wooden bed, a great oak chest and a wooden stool, all made as if to last for ever. A few very clean cooking-things were on the stove, and fishing-lines and nets were hanging from wooden pegs on the walls. The second room held no furniture but a bench and a big handloom for weaving. There was some grand strong canvas being made upon it, and, as I looked at it, I guessed suddenly that here were being made the sails for the ship.

Without knowing why, I hurried out of the cabin into the sunshine. Leaning on the gate into the cornfield, as if he had been there all the time, an old man stood watching me. He had steel-grey curly hair and very dark blue eyes. The skin of his face was clear walnut. He might have been any age from fifty to a hundred. His clothes were of some strong homespun cloth, probably made on the loom where he was making the sails. The shoes on his bare brown feet were of woven string with soles of thick rope. With his arrival the whole place seemed to have sprung to life. He was accompanied by three sheep, and two pigs snuffled in the ground close by. A dog, impassive as its master, lay beside the gate, half opening his eyes, as if he had been waked from sleep.

Somehow I could make no apology for having gone into his cottage. I asked him where to land eastwards along the coast and for the nearest anchorage sheltered from the north-west. He told me what I wanted gravely, and with a curious air of taking his words one by one out of a lumber-room and dusting them before use. I tried to get eggs and butter from him, but he said he had no eggs and never made more butter than he needed. I should get some from the forester at Palli or at Luidja, near the anchorage. I asked him about the pier. Once upon a time there had been people here and timber traffic?

"Yes, but that was a long time ago, and the people have all gone away."

"Was it then that you began building the ship?"

"Yes; that was when I began building the ship."

His dark-blue eyes, watching me, but indifferent as the sea itself, invited no more questions. I turned back by the path under the great ship so many times larger than his cottage, and found myself oddly hurried as I pushed our little boat into the water and rowed away. I could just catch the sunlight splashes on the body of the ship among the trees. Would she ever be finished? And what then? What had he planned as he worked at her year after year? Would he die before his dream came true, or before he knew that the dreaming was the better part of it?

But the sunlight faded and the wind had freshened, and for a time I thought no more about him, for we had enough to do with our own ship.

BALTIC PORT TO SPITHAMN

SEPTEMBER 7th. Barometer 30.25. Wind at dawn S.W., slight. We sailed at 7 a.m. without incident, except that in pushing our way out along the eastern quay the sharp point of our long boathook (a Dvina lumberman's pole with a really sharp spike on the end, used for handling floating logs) stuck fast in the wooden piles and the pole remained quivering there, like the Trojan's spear in the wooden sides of that barrack of a horse, until it was extracted by a good fellow who climbed down for it and brought it round to the narrow harbour mouth and gave it back to us as we rounded the pierhead. We then had a fair wind out of the bight into which we had so laboriously tacked the night before last. It was a fair wind, but a very light one. It shifted to the S., and at 8.20 we were at the mouth of the bay on a line between the point of East Roogö and Pakerort.

We bore up to pass as near as might be West Roogö Point, where the English charts are right in marking "a conspicuous tree". The tree is a very little one, but it is the only one on that desolate promontory; no, not quite the only one, for, as we came nearer, we saw that its successor was already being prepared. A little tree, exactly like the first, is growing close to it, so that when the old one dies or is blown away, another shall be conspicuous in its stead. The tree is dead; long live the tree! – and the charts shall need no correction. Would that similar precautions had been taken in other places!

It was a glorious morning of brilliant sunshine, but the wind grew less and less, and what there was shifting against us. At 9.45 we were off West Roogö spar-buoy, close by the wind and heading W.S.W. and $^{1}/_{2}$ W. At eleven we were still between West Roogö and Grasgrund, but were now on the starboard tack and heading SW. and $\frac{1}{2}$ W., the wind having shifted northerly. The rock of Grasgrund, which had been visible on our way eastwards, was now not alone, and a considerable island had appeared above water. A fishing-boat had tied up to this amphibious place and a couple of lads were sunning themselves on ground far out at sea which is almost always a foot or two under water. Far inshore, behind Roogö Island, we sighted a cutter which had probably spent the night by the little village of Wichterpal, now slowly working westwards like ourselves. We held her all day.

At noon the wind increased a little, coming from W.N.W. We set the mizen staysail and tried to pretend to ourselves that we were moving quite fast. We were able to keep more or less on our course, and, as the afternoon wore on, Odensholm from being a row of spots on the horizon became a visible definite island, with a lighthouse at one end and a cutter's mast at the other, near by a shed or two.

The barometer, however, was falling. We were bound for the Worms Nukke Channel, which is not lit, and we had no longer the smallest chance of getting there by daylight. Once round the point of Spithamn we should have a long way to go for shelter. Looking S. towards the land we saw that the cutter which had sailed abeam of us from the Roogö islands was far inshore, clearly making for the hither side of Spithamn, where a schooner was already at anchor. We made up our minds to trust to "local knowledge" and do the same. We altered our course, and having the wind free, stood straight in for the two ships, encouraged by seeing the cutter round up close by the schooner and lower her sails just as we put the helm up. We sailed in close by the rocky side of Spithamn and saw the six windmills (five according to the charts, but really six) on the little hill. Boats, loaded gunwale-deep in firewood, were coming off shore to the schooner, just as I had seen last year off the northern coast of Dagö, where also is no harbour. The schooners anchor off shore. The wood is carried into the water on little carts, then packed into boats, leaving just room for a couple of boys, who on reaching the ship throw the wood up log by log to the captain, his wife, his men and his children, who stow it in the hold. If the wind blows on shore, loading is interrupted and the schooners put to sea, returning when a change of wind brings smooth water.

As we slipped along towards them, the captain of the cutter gave us the use of his local knowledge in the nick of time by waving us eastward of a shallow patch which, in the failing light, we had not observed immediately on our bows. We were using the lead, but had no warning of it until the captain's hail and wave, instantly obeyed, saved us by a few yards. When we had cleared the shoal he waved again, and five minutes afterwards we were at anchor beside the others. We were three – the firewood-loading schooner, big and quite new, the elderly cutter, about twice our own size, and the little *Racundra*, shielded from the W. by Spithamn Point (Spint Head on English charts), more or less shielded from the E. by the distant islands of Roogö, but open to the N. and N.W., with nothing but the little island of Odensholm between us and the coast of Sweden, near two hundred miles away. Not a very good anchorage, but, as I reasoned, the schooner, being worse than ourselves in working to windward, would clear out in plenty of time to give us warning, and the skipper of the cutter would hardly be putting the covers on his sails and be getting ready to go ashore if he had expected anything very bad during the night.

We slung the dinghy overboard with a tackle, and the Cook and I went ashore to see what we could of Spithamn before it grew too dark. An elderly man in grey homespuns saw us coming and walked from his cottage just above high-water mark down to the shingle. He helped us to pull up the dinghy, and fastened the painter to a thwart of a boat of his own that was lying well out of reach of the waves. Then, having in this manner made us his guests, he spoke to us in German, in Swedish, in Esthonian and in Russian, apologizing for not knowing more than a few words of English, and those words of the sea and unlikely for the moment to be of much use. He was very pleased to know so many languages, delighted that we could answer him a word or two in each of them, inquired politely in Swedish which language we preferred to talk, and finding that Russian came easiest to us went on with our talk in that. He was a Swede and his name was Anders Ringberg. He took the Cook into his charge and sold her milk, potatoes, and little very salt fish, which he swore had been caught the previous day and were hardly salt at all. For this gross error, however, he atoned by making her a present of some cranberries and giving me copies of two Swedish newspapers, issued specially for the Swedes of the Esthonian islands, these relics of the old Swedish colonization; the Reval one a typical local newspaper, with its little scrap of gossip about Odensholm, about Runö, about Worms, about each one of the Swedish settlements, so that no one of its purchasers should fail to find in it something of peculiar interest to himself. It even recorded with proper solemnity the rare visits of yachts to the outlying islets. Anders Ringberg was very disappointed that we could not play the harmonium, for he had one in his house and had made sure at once that we, as educated people from far countries, would be able to do wonderful things with it. Hemp was growing in his garden, and he told us that the men of Spithamn not only build their own boats (they had built the big schooner that was lying beside *Racundra*), but spun and wove the hemp, making nets, ropes, fishing-lines, and very stout clothes for their sea-going.

I went for a walk up the little hill to see the windmills, of the same form as those on Roogö Island. From the hill I could see down through a gap in the pinewoods to the shore on the other side of the promontory, where in the trees another schooner was building. Here, so I learnt, there is better anchorage, but the way into it is extremely dangerous for those who do not know the rocks. There is, of course, no detailed chart of the place.

Coming down the hill again, I walked through the village of Spithamn, a village of stout log huts, with, as on Roogö, fine pigs walking about the narrow lanes, and everywhere fishing-nets drying. Some of the houses were rudely painted with ochre, but most were the natural colour of the weather-beaten wood, the ends of the logs dove-tailed across each other at the corners. One small hut caught my eye from a long way off with the word "York" upon it in big white letters. I came near to it and found that I was looking at the carved name-board of a ship built into the house. There was the green painted scroll-work, and in the middle of it, carved deeply from the wood, those big white letters on which, no doubt, many waves had beat before the ship that carried them went ashore and was broken up, to the profit of the natives, on the rocks beyond the point. An English ship, or may be an American, and she must have been wrecked here a long time ago, as many others have been wrecked, for not Anders Ringberg nor anyone else could tell me anything about her.

Down on the beach the men had stopped work for the night. The last of the boats which had been carrying firewood to the schooner came in and grounded. A wire rope was shackled to a ring on the waterline under her bows, and I lent a hand at winding her up over fir rollers by means of a primitive capstan deeply bedded in the beach. Two small men of Spithamn, aged about eight, I suppose, were early beginning their inevitable career, sailing against each other two beautiful models of their fathers' broad-bowed schooners. They were wading in the water, and one of them brought his model ashore to show me. Every detail of the rigging was there, and the hull was built like the ships themselves, decked, with a hatch amidships, a small square, half-sunk deckhouse aft, the wheel behind that, the sails broad and not high, with large topsails, two jibs and a staysail.

The skipper of the cutter had made several trips to the shore and back with things he had brought in his ship. He was now unloading his little boat for the last time. He had brought ashore sacks of coal for the winter, much other gear, and a heavy, iron-bound ancient trunk. He told me of the harbourage there is in Odensholm, and said he always left his cutter there for the winter, when ice makes sailing impossible. "There, no matter what may be, the ice can never touch her." He himself spends the winter ashore here in Spithamn. He asked if we were not the boat that had come to Reval during

OUR NEIGHBOUR AT SPITHAMN.

TWO SMALL SAILORS, WITH A MODEL OF HER.

the gale of a fortnight before, said he had been sheltering in Reval at the time, and paid *Racundra* almost as many compliments as that stout little ship deserved. With these compliments warming my heart, as compliments to *Racundra* always do warm it, I made my way back along the shore to the dinghy, where the Cook had already arrived with her parcels. We rowed back through smooth water, for the wind had fallen altogether, so that I was glad we were not drifting about on the other side of the point; and after we had had supper and decided that Anders Ringberg ought not to have mistaken his fish for fish caught yesterday, we smoked in the cockpit and looked towards the village. It was nine o'clock. There was not a light to be seen. Everyone in the place had gone to bed. The blinking light on Roogö showed far away, and the light on Odensholm, and we could just see another behind the trees on the point warning the "Yorks" of these days not to come to provide name-boards for the Spithamn houses. Schooner and cutter were in perfect darkness, so *Racundra* ran her riding light up the forestay to serve alike for herself and her big sisters, and we turned in and slept.

After midnight I went on deck and found the wind easterly, the moon high, clouds overhead moving from the S., and the sea nearly calm.

SPITHAMN TO RAMSHOLM

SEPTEMBER 8th. Barometer 30. We had a fine night at our Spithamn anchorage. I went on deck two or three times, but those high clouds at midnight had been true prophets; the wind had changed to the S., *Racundra* swung with her nose to the land and at dawn the sea was scarcely rippled. Those six windmills on the skyline of the hill were now on our starboard bow, and we had a kindly little wind to take us out to sea again and round the point, after which it would be clean in our faces, for I had set my heart on going due S. and taking *Racundra* through the channel between Worms and the mainland, instead of back by the way we had come through the deeper, wider channel between Worms and Dagö. The *Baltic Pilot* says: "Hapsal [whither we were bound] can be approached from the northward by the channel between Wormsö and Nukke Peninsula, but it is so narrow and winding that the navigation is difficult even with local knowledge, assisted by the buoys." There is no need to explain to any yachtsman the passionate desire of everyone on board to take *Racundra* through that way. I had had the chart on the wall of my room all winter, and was sure that, given a fair wind, there would be no difficulty about it. So we decided to make no change of plan, but to beat S., get into the shelter of the land as near the channel as we could, and, if the wind should change, why, then rejoice and run through to Hapsal.

The wind did not change, and blew from the S., shifting in its most annoying manner, so that every time we went about we found ourselves pointing nothing like so well as we had hoped. We spent twelve tedious hours in making the dozen miles between Spithamn and the entrance to the channel,

sailing, of course, a very much greater distance as we
zigzagged against that fitful wind. As soon as we rounded
Spithamn at about half-past seven in the morning we met
three schooners racing northwards neck and neck; and after
that throughout the day a long procession of sailing vessels
with their booms wide out, schooners goose-winged, came
rejoicing from the S., whither we were painfully beating.
Sturdy Wormsö schooners, a few clean, smartly painted
Finns, cutters running home to Reval, others bound for
Kaspervik, more than twenty sail we counted, and we did
not begin to count until many had already dropped hull-down
to northward of us. Ship after ship made a fair and
unforgivable picture. In a sailing vessel beating against the
wind, meeting other sailing vessels running free, you know
the whole bitterness of the poor man picking the crumbs
from the floor at the rich man's feast. And looking at the
men on board the running vessels as they idly lean on their
railings watching your slow progress as they flash by, it is hard
not to believe that they are feeling all the selfish complaisance
of the rich.

It was smooth-water sailing, and the Cook made jam with
the cranberries that had been Anders Ringberg's conscience
money in the matter of the salt fish. The Ancient was much
interested in the jam-making, and, while I was steering,
I could hear them in the galley discussing the far more
valuable art of making marmalade, an art that we discovered
for ourselves slowly and by means of accidents, as Charles
Lamb's Chinaman learnt the delights of roast pork through
the burning of his house. The recipe for marmalade in
Racundra is as follows: First buy your oranges; then eat your
oranges, but do not throw the peel into the sea. Then boil the
peel. Then – but here I must revert to our actual discovery,
which was made on *Kittiwake* and not in *Racundra*, which is
a far steadier boat. Then (in *Kittiwake*) make an inadvertent
movement from one side of the boat to the other and upset
the whole boiling into the bilge. Collect the orange peel from
the bottom boards and stew once more with plenty of sugar,
when the result will be indistinguishable from the best

English marmalade. The important discovery, apart from the fact that by this process you can both eat your oranges and have your marmalade, was the upsetting. Until that event we had not known that the water of the first boiling should be poured off, and the final stewing done with fresh water, and this last is the whole secret of marmalade. Having once discovered it, we never troubled again to rock the boat, and can make just as good marmalade in *Racundra* as in the diminutive and unstable *Kittiwake*.

Jam-making was in full steam when at eleven I got a good fix of our position, with Telness beacons in line on the mainland to the E. of us and Saxbiness lighthouse far away on the island of Worms, bearing S.W. by W. After that we took turns in keeping a pretty careful look-out, for many outlying rocks and shoals explain the unwillingness of the *Baltic Pilot* to give any directions for this passage except the advice not to try it. By 2.45 we were about two hundred yards from the Savinova spar-buoy. We went about and, with a slight change of wind, pointed on the starboard tack S.E. towards the mainland, going about again when we came near the rocks awash north of Telness Point. It had long been clear that we could not hope to get through that day, and I began to search the chart for a possible anchorage and decided to leave the fairway close to the entrance to the channel and to anchor between two shoals north of Ramsholm. Accordingly, after passing close by the buoys that mark the Sgibneva bank, we steered S.E., keeping the lead going; and at 6.30 while it was still light enough to see that we had a sandy bottom, let go in two fathoms of water, lowering our sails but not taking the halyards off or putting the covers on, so as to be able to clear out at a moment's notice. Just as we had everything snug, I saw a cutter, the last of that long procession, coming with a fair wind from the S. out from between the mainland and Worms, through the channel I wanted to enter in the morning. With the long-distance glasses I saw her pass between stakes, and was able to take a bearing of them and identify them on the chart. If need should be and the wind should come from the N., we should be able at least to get so far in the direction of shelter.

However, the wind did not change, but rather strengthened from the S. We had warm jam "to our supper", as we say in Yorkshire, and lay very snug and quiet in a place rather beastly from a sailor's point of view (because it gave us so little elbow-room in case of change of wind), but very fine to look at. Away to the S.W. was the wooded island of Worms. S. of us was the desolate point of Ramsholm, and far away eastward was the low-lying mainland. As dark closed in upon us there was not a single light to be seen. The Worms Lighthouse at Saxbiness was at the other side of the island and hidden from us. Odensholm had sunk below the horizon to the N. There was no light on shore in cottage or farm. *Racundra* tasted all the isolation of Noah's Ark, alone as the flood receded and showed the peaks and uplands of a depopulated earth. She was, however, aground upon no Ararat, but swung gently to her anchor in a little natural harbour, every mole and breakwater of which was hidden under water.

RAMSHOLM TO HAPSAL THROUGH THE
NUKKE CHANNEL

I had left the lead overboard as a means of telling whether our anchor held, and three or four times in the night I went on deck to have a look at the lead-line. Once, when the wind had shifted and we had swung a quarter of a circle, the line stretching far out on our beam gave me a bit of a fright, but I went forward and found I could easily hold the boat by one hand on the chain. I took in the lead and dropped it again, and satisfied myself that we were not moving, and finally turned in so thoroughly reassured that I slept until six and was very unwilling to get up even then. However, the wind began to make a rowdy hullabaloo overhead, and at half-past six I turned out sleepily to find that it was blowing hard from the S.E. dead against us.

I had been told that the channel was impossible for a sailing vessel against the wind and that the local sailors never attempt it, but wait at the entrance till the wind will take them through, this being the reason why yesterday we had met such a number of sail all together. Still, we had made our present anchorage against this same wind, and I decided to try to get through, making up my mind beforehand that there should be no false squeamishness about dropping back in case we should find ourselves engaged on a hopeless bit of work.

One can always find a good enough reason for doing anything that one has made up one's mind to do. In this case I had a perfect one, quite apart from the fact that we did not like staying where we were, and that the jam had been so good that we had eaten all the bread and could get no more till we should come to Hapsal. There was a reason *pro* and a reason *contra* – everything, in fact, that the human mind requires when it is putting up a pretence of being logical. The wind looked like continuing, but, so far as I could see through the long-distance glasses, there was not yet much current about the spar-buoys, which, however, were standing very high out of the water, tatters of seaweed clinging to them far above the waterline showing their more normal depth. I was sure of two things: the first, that a strong current would be setting against us out of the Sound within a very few hours, and the second, that I should have to deal with depths abnormally low. The first outweighed the second, and at seven in the morning our anchor was up and hanging at our bows, ready to drop at any moment in case of need, and we were off warily back to the fairway, the lead going all the time in two fathoms of water. Then we beat up towards the two spar-buoys that mark the entrance to the passage.

The men on a cutter whirling out of the channel with the wind behind them looked at us as if they thought we were mad and shrugged their shoulders with expression. But, though *Racundra* is not good at beating as compared with racing yachts, she is better against the wind than any of the local cutters and schooners, and, when we set her at it this morning, she seemed to know she was expected to do her best, and did it. There was a toughish wind, too, and that always suits her. With less wind we should not have tried it. At the same time, we left nothing to chance and took no risks of her missing stays, which, in this narrow way between rocks and sharply shoaling banks, would have meant almost inevitable disaster. I had sweated over the chart till I knew it pretty well by heart, and indeed only looked at it twice, and that when we were already through the actual channel and were out again in more or less open water, looking for the buoys and beacons that show the way into Hapsal Bay. I therefore set the Ancient at the tiller and went forward myself with the lead-line handy, though as a matter of fact there was never time to use it and it would have been useless, because there is no gradual shoaling. You are either in the channel with three fathoms of water or out of the channel with a fathom or less, or on a rock

HAPSAL JETTY (SHOWING LEADING BEACONS).

DRYING OUT.

with no more than a couple of feet. My real business forward was to deal with the staysail in getting her quickly about and to con the little ship in without, if I could help it, communicating to the Ancient any of the doubts with which I was myself beset.

I kept my eyes on the sticks which here serve as spar-buoys, on the colour of the water and on the bottom, often only too visible, and shouted "Ready about" in a tone as near as possible that in which those words are spoken when we are at sea and have the whole Baltic to make mistakes in. At first the Ancient was just a little bit petulant at the frequency of our tacks, but we touched once with the centreboard from hanging on an extra second, once only, and from that moment he was perfect and everything worked in the delirious, exciting manner of tight-rope walking. He knew then that we really were on a tight-rope, and that this was not an example of my ridiculous preference for imagining, when navigating, that *Racundra* has the draught of a big ship. We swung round as the words were out of my mouth; I had the staysail aback till the mainsail filled, and we were off again, rushing from side to side of the channel, making a bit every time, creeping up in hurried zigzags, a dozen or so between each buoy. The chart that I had read so often in the winter took visible solid shape as we moved. There was Mereholm; there those rocks awash; there two windmills on Nukke; there, at last, the buoy with a ball and two brooms, bases apart, on the top. The brooms are not there, but that must be the buoy none the less.

It is hard enough to give an idea of how things looked. At first, of course, there was the open sea behind us, and we were pushing our way in between the wooded island of Worms and the low, grass-patched and rocky mainland. The two were always a good distance apart, but outcrops from both of them were close to us either above or under water, and at times it was difficult to preserve one's faith in chart knowledge and to sail so near those brown rocks with such a space of open water on the other side. How much simpler to sail boldly up the middle. And then, on the other tack, just a few score yards, often less, and there were more rocks under the water, or pale green shallows splashed with dark, and we were thankfully about again and scuttling back towards the brown lumps that at least were out of water and less secretive in their villainy. And yet, what a stretch of water! and round *Racundra* would go again, the wavelets foaming under her bows, and so on, to and fro, to and fro, each time gaining a little southwards against the wind, through gusts of which I had to yell to be heard by the Ancient at the tiller.

I had enjoyed following the intricate Moon Sound channel from Paternoster through by the Erik Stone and Harry Island to the open sea, but there big ships could go, and we had a margin of yards and sometimes far more, in case we left it for a moment. Here there was no margin at all. We were ourselves drawing with centreboard down (as we had to have it down for beating against the wind) more than most of the small coasters who alone use this channel. It was incredibly exciting, the more so that as we proceeded, and time went on and the wind still blew, there was visibly growing current against us from the S. through the channel. It became a race between us and the current and the wind. Could we get through to the open and round into the bay of Hapsal before the wind had made the current so great that we could not hold against it?[1] Each spar-buoy left astern was a separate triumph, and I would hardly let myself believe that we had left the worst of the channel behind us until the view before us had already widened, and we could see far into the broad Sound, where hull-down were three goose-winged schooners hurrying from the S. before the wind that for them was a friendly ally, the same wind that *Racundra*, sailing from the N., had had to meet and conquer. Now, after just four hours of frenzied beating, we were making longer tacks, keeping our eyes on two tall beacons on the mainland on the southern side of Hapsal Bay, already within the mouth of the inlet, and

---

[1] I am told by hydrographers that it is probably incorrect to say that the wind causes the current through these channels. They say that wind and current are alike caused by pressure, or lack of it, elsewhere. To the simple sailormen of these parts, however, the fact remains that wind from the south brings current from the south, wind from the west brings a rise of water in the otherwise tideless Sound, wind from the east lowers the waters there, and in writing about these phenomena I have written as they speak.

watching to bring two other beacons in line under Hapsal town with its church and ruined castle. Those two beacons, one on shore and one on a bit of a rock almost awash, would lead us safely between the shallows towards the little Hapsal harbour, on the quay of which again are two other beacons, which, taken in line, help little ships through the last few hundred yards of their passage. We shifted from the line of the first pair to the line of the second, found the spar-buoys that supplement these land signs, and then, sailing E. with the wind free, fairly foamed from buoy to buoy until at noon we rounded up and anchored beside two small trading cutters about a cable's length from Hapsal pierhead.

*   *   *   *   *

Here we lay for two nights, waiting for a fair wind, and used the intervening day of bright sunshine for the drying of bedding and mattresses and for a visit to the town which is some little way from the jetty. Indeed, as you approach Hapsal from the sea, the jetty, with the tall white granary behind it, looks like an island, for the narrow strip of land that connects it with the town is flat and low. The town itself is grouped round a low hillock on which is a ruined castle, which has, so we learnt, its ghosts and its Hounds of Hell guarding hidden treasure, all indeed that is necessary and fitting for a ruin in a popular watering-place.

The castle was the residence of the German bishops who, during the thirteenth century, made themselves the first foreign rulers of Esthonia. The revolting Ests tried in vain to take it in 1334. Two hundred years and more after that it was taken by the Swedes. They did not hold it for long, for the Swedish officer commanding had no money to pay his troops, and so, in those good old days of private initiative, pawned the castle to his soldiers on the understanding that, if their pay did not arrive by the next Midsummer's Day, they could sell the castle to whom they chose, on condition that the buyer should be a Christian, but should not be either the Russian Tsar or Bishop Magnus, who had married a niece of Ivan the Terrible.

The soldiers did not get their pay and did actually sell the
castle for forty thousand talers to Ungern, who was acting
viceroy for the King of Denmark. Next year the Russians took
it for nothing and without meeting any resistance, for which
reason the Danish leader, Stark, was duly executed in
Arensburg. Ten years later the Russians, after a fight, lost it to
the Swedes, and in 1628 the Swedish King, improving on the
commercial methods of the Swedish soldiers, sold it for
66,830 talers to a Field-Marshal, whose son died in the utmost
poverty after his father's purchase had been quietly
re-appropriated by the Crown, who perhaps were thinking of
selling it again. But the Swedes held on to the property too
long, for before they tried to sell it a third time, Peter the Great
in 1710 made it Russian, and Russian it remained until 1918,
when it was occupied by the Germans, on whose departure the
Ests came at last into their own.

We had this ruin to see and, besides that, needed bread,
milk, meat and matches, and had set our hearts on a cabbage,
which we had not been able to find in Baltic Port. So after
bathing in the early morning, we walked in over the low slip
of land, that would certainly be covered at high water if this
were not a tideless sea, and came to the town – a little town
with winding streets of stone and wooden houses, twisting
about round the shallow inlets of water, and from one
promontory to another in a manner most confusing to a
stranger. We had some difficulty in finding the shops, which
were, as everyone told us, in the middle of the town. The
Esthonians are an admirable, tenacious people, but in all the
years of my acquaintance with them I have never met one who
knew how to tell me the way. They will point vaguely in the
wrong direction, or, if they point in the right direction, will
tell you, as a landmark, to look out for a tree with a broken
branch among several hundreds all with broken branches,
instead of mentioning a large, obvious barn which a blind man
could not miss. Here, in Hapsal, we found the further
difficulty that the cosmopolitan season was over and that
therefore everybody had ceased to understand any language
but Esthonian. I was there once for a few days earlier in the

summer, when most people seemed to know both Russian and German. Now it was as if every linguist in the place had gone into hibernation till next spring. We did, however, at last come out in the middle of the town, where we found two hotels. We tried both. In one a man was viciously tuning a piano. In the other there was a gramophone. In neither did we see any visitors besides ourselves, and in both we were told at once that the season was over. Indeed we were told so by everyone with whom we spoke, even by the baker from whom we bought the bread, as much as to say that we had no business to be there. I got the impression that the town was quite consciously recovering itself, drawing a long breath and enjoying its nationality after the alien but profitable bustle of the summer.

In summer Hapsal is crowded with visitors, who, for the most part, do not live in the hotels, but rent the little houses, or parts of them, at so much "for the season". It is not as in England, where whole families go to the seaside for a tumultuous fortnight or month of holiday. Here, the men plant out their wives and children at Hapsal for the summer, to get brown, take mud baths and cure imaginary diseases, while they run down from Reval by train for the week ends. There is a floating restaurant on the inland lake, and great consumption of vanilla ices, besides open-air concerts, regattas in hired boats – in fact, opportunities for all that such visitors demand.

When *Racundra* sailed in there, all this maelstrom of amusement was still. The idle crowds of hypochondriac rheumatics taking the baths and impatiently exchanging symptoms had disappeared. The little town was itself again, and, if I were to stay there, the back end of the year is certainly the time that I should choose. The tiny market under the castle was quietly busy in the morning, as no doubt it has been since the Middle Ages. We met there women from the country and the islands in their local costume – bright red bodices, black accordion-pleated skirts, with red stockings, short white socks over the red stockings and black shoes with strips of black leather criss-cross over the white socks. And though the visitors were gone the boats remained, and, for the crew of *Racundra*, these boats compete with the ruins as the things of most interest in Hapsal.

I should explain that beyond the pier and the town and those flat promontories is a huge stretch of shallow water, on which the men of Hapsal take their summer visitors sailing. This inland sea is nowhere more than a very few feet deep, and a special type of boat, unlike any others on the Esthonian coast, has been evolved for sailing on it. I have a reproduction of an old drawing showing that boats something like these were in existence in the very early nineteenth century, if not earlier. They are shaped a little like the shallow wherries of the Norfolk Broads, but are, of course, much smaller. They have a fair-sized cabin right forward, with a big well for the passengers and a small well right aft for the steersman, who from that position controls the sails. The mainsail is extremely high and they are sloop-rigged. They have neither centreboards nor lee-boards, but, drawing not more than a couple of feet of water, they sail in the most remarkable manner both off and by the wind.

HAPSAL TO HELTERMAA (ISLAND OF DAGÖ)

SEPTEMBER 11th. Barometer 29.9. The wind was still against us this morning, shifting between W. and S.W., but a whole day lying at anchor had made us determined to move, if only to get through the difficult bit between the Rukeraga and Odroraga reefs, or, if we should fail to do that, at least to get to anchorage at Estholm, ready to slip through the moment the wind should change. We got our anchor at 7.30 and, slowly tacking, passed by the pierhead near enough to learn that the fishermen thereon, who had come before the dawn, had caught two little silver fish between them. Then we began with infinite labour to retrace, as far as the black-and-white buoy where the channel from Nukke and Worms joins that from the S., the course which we had run so merrily with the wind free two days before.

The sun was behind the Hapsal beacons, and in the glare over the water they were quite invisible, so we just felt our way out, tacking from spar-buoy to spar-buoy, the Ancient in the bows singing out when he saw the bottom coming up to meet us. The Cook was busy with the breakfast, two Primuses going at once, steam from the porridge coming up the companion-way together with the rich dark smell of frying bacon. At nine we reached the first of the main buoys and at ten minutes past ten we were at the third, round which the channel turns to the S. Here we brought *Racundra* to the wind and hove to while we hauled the dinghy on board. We then tacked on southwards. It was a wearisome business, but we were all keen to go on, for with the wind backing to the S.W. we had a good hope of being able to point straight through the narrow alleyway of buoys between the reefs. We went as close as we dared to the Odroraga and saw its wicked line just below the surface of the water, and at one point a little strip of it, pale red above the wavelets, with seabirds huddled together upon it. We stood away then for Estholm, where are the beginnings and the ruins of a fine harbour, warehouses and quays alike broken by the war, wrecks of half-sunk pontoons lifting desperately into the air and a forlorn crane. A little cutter was at anchor close by the piers. We had watched her through the glasses, picking her way in with lowered foresail and dropped peak. Away to the E., with the wind behind her, a fine schooner was coming easily through the passage by the Rukeraga beacon. We went about and sailed close-hauled to meet her.

The beacon is fixed on the northern end of a low strip of rock, just above the level of the water. The *Baltic Pilot*, by the way, like the German chart, gives a most inaccurate picture of it, suggesting a low pyramid supporting a square. It may have been so once upon a time. Now it is a tall openwork obelisk, visible from a great distance, and easily recognizable from a few miles away because of the big conical stones which lie near it. Just N. of it and running E. and W. is a narrow lane of four pairs of spar-buoys. The channel between them is not a stone's-throw across, and, as there are rocks and stone shallows just outside the line of the buoys on either side, beating through it is impossible.

We met the schooner, envying her speed and favourable wind, and reaching the first pair of buoys, found we could just point through the channel. We passed the first three pairs of buoys with no difficulty, and were just rejoicing in having got through a ticklish bit of sailing when I noticed that, though we were heading by compass as before, the wind had fallen a little, and the last pair of buoys were slipping slowly southwards. I brought *Racundra's* head a fraction up. It made no difference. We were already caught in the current, which, sweeping up along the far side of the reefs, touched us here, whereas it had been imperceptible during the first three-quarters of the passage. There was nothing to be done. There was neither time nor room to beat. We were already close upon the last pair of buoys, and we were on the wrong side of the northern one. I shouted forward and the Ancient stood by with the anchor as a last resource, while we stood on, our hearts in our mouths. The buoy was abeam of us and visibly slipping away. It was on our quarter. It was astern. There came a puff of wind and *Racundra* answered it at once, and a moment later the Ancient looked happily over his shoulder. "Deep water," he called, and we knew that we were out in the Moon Sound proper, where big steamers find their way and where beacons are lit at night. Now we cared for nothing. I let *Racundra* fall a point off the wind and she brisked up like a horse after a feed of oats. The wind backed a little more and she pointed W. by S. and even W.S.W. That, however, was the best that she could do, and we were not yet far enough from the reefs to put her about on the other tack. So we held on, watching the southern shore of Worms and recognizing far before us the low coast of Dagö Island and Pihalep church spire, that is a good guide from afar to the pleasant little harbour of Heltermaa.

Then the wind strengthened and fell away, strengthened and fell away from the S.W., the short unpleasing sea of the Moon Sound got up, and the admirable *Racundra* began to show us that we had been wrong in boasting that she did not roll. She rolled abominably. The main boom swung from side to side with mighty bangs, until I lashed it to the lee backstay tackle. The mizen boom swung on unheeded. Things were very unpleasant, and, as we looked back to the tall Rukeraga beacon, seeming now as if it floated in the water, it was clear enough that we were making very little southing. If that was so in this part of the Sound, if the current was so strong here, it would be very much worse in the narrows to the S., and, anxious as we were to get along, we had no sort of wish to spend the night in vainly beating to and fro against wind and current together. Just then the two little steamers from Hapsal, the *Endla* and the *Hiumaa*, rivals for the exiguous Dagö trade, passed us bound cheerfully for Heltermaa. I had been in Heltermaa before, and knew it for a picturesque place, one of the smallest good harbours in the world. There was that church on the horizon, a fine mark to steer by; and, after all, we reasoned, if the wind should change we should be able to consider the visit to Heltermaa merely as a longer tack. We could lose nothing by going there. So we made

"RACUNDRA" AT HELTERMAA (DAGÖ ISLAND).

HELTERMAA HARBOUR TODAY.

up our minds to hold on until either the wind should change or we should come to Heltermaa. The wind did not change, so we came to Heltermaa just before sunset. At 6.15 we warped in round *Endla's* stern, nearly carrying away her flagstaff as we did so, owing to the energy with which we were helped by the men of Heltermaa, and found ourselves in very snug quarters for the night.

There was room in Heltermaa harbour for the tiny *Hiumaa*, one open fishing-boat, a dinghy, *Racundra*, the *Endla* and a schooner of small size. But *Endla* was tied up outside the harbour proper, across the end of the pierhead, and the schooner was at anchor. The fishing-boat, *Racundra* and *Hiumaa* filled all available quay berths. A young man in uniform, who was, I think, coastguard, soldier and harbourmaster, came on board and enthusiastically pencilled the date of *Racundra's* arrival on her papers. Then, as it looked like rain, we put the covers on the sails; and, while the Cook and the Ancient began to make supper, I set out with a milk-can, an egg-basket and a string bag to do some provisioning.

A hundred yards or so from the harbour is a so-called inn, that was once a Russian posting-station where you could hire horses, at so many kopecks per mile per horse, to take you across the island. It is still called an inn, and people do sleep on sacks of straw there, if they are on their way to Hapsal and the Sound is too rough for the little steamer. Its landlord, who has or had some official connection with the harbour, talks only Esthonian, nor does his wife talk any other language. My dealings with them were not easy. I tried English. I tried Russian. These failing, I took a long breath and asked them for milk in Esthonian.

"Piima," I said, and waved my milk-can.

"Ei ole piima," they replied in chorus.

All right. If they had no milk I would try for eggs.

"Muna," I said, and the good woman scuttled off as if she were a hen herself and came back with a lot of very little eggs.

"Kui palio maksap?" said I.

"Kumme munat (ten eggs)," said the woman, counting on her fingers. "Nelli kument mark."

"Forty marks." I had only a note for a hundred, and they had no change or very little, so they gave me ten marks back and a number of new white loaves.

That was all they could do, but that was not enough. They pointed up the road towards the forest, and I went to the next house, which turned out to be the school-house. I found a young woman in a pink cotton dress sitting on the back of a desk. She was the schoolmistress and this an idle hour. I tried English, and she turned the colour of a ripe apple.

"I know English," she said, and promptly, in her embarrassment, forgot all she knew.

I dare say she reads Shakespeare. I think it highly likely that she teaches English. She understood perfectly when I explained that I wanted milk; but when she tried to answer, it was as if someone held her tongue by the roots and muffled her brain. By now, I am sure, she has thought out the speech she should have made. At the time she was struck dumb, and, coming to the doorstep, could only point up the road into the forest, turn redder and redder, so that her pink cotton dress looked almost white, and stammer, "House, house, house, house . . ." and then, with a flash of memory, "YELLOW house." So I thanked her and she fled away back into her schoolroom, while I went on towards the trees, looking for a yellow house.

I found the yellow house; but the woman therein, who talked Esthonian to me, exhausted herself in explaining that they had only one cow and were ten in family. She directed me to another house where she said they were few in family but had two cows. I found that house; but the woman in it said that I could have milk only when the cows should come home, and that they were not expected home before eight o'clock. However, she directed me to another house.

Here I found a little elderly woman with a face wrinkled all over, the most charming wrinkles, so that when she smiled every line in her face took part in the smile; and she, while explaining that she had no milk, would not let me go, but held me firmly by my jersey, and called for her husband to come out and look. To me she said, "We have no milk," but to him, "Here is an Englishman," and held me firmly till he came, a long, thin, smiling fellow who somehow reminded me of John Masefield, I accordingly felt friendly towards him, and perhaps I reminded him of someone, for he seemed to feel friendship for me, and took me by the arm and led me to a stake hedge, where he pulled out a stake to let me through, and said, "Over there is a house with a little white barn, and there lives a Russian man, and he has good cows, and will certainly give you milk."

So I wandered on into the forest and came to a house with a little pigsty beside it with a glass window, the only pigsty with a glass window that I can remember to have seen. And beyond that, sure enough, was a house, a log cabin, with a tiny barn, and the barn was whitewashed. And here I spoke to the woman of that house in Russian; but she did not understand me, and called to her husband, who came from the potato-bed, wearing his shirt outside his trousers in the Russian fashion.

With him, of course, I had a good talk and great difficulty in coming to business. He told me he had come here as a soldier in the Russian service thirty years ago, and had married a wife and lived here ever since. "Yet, if I were to ask some of them from our village, by Poltava, to help me till this ground, they would laugh at me, for they would say there was nothing to be got out of it, and indeed in Poltava is the black earth and here is nothing but stone; but now I am fifty years old and a little more, and I am not too well, and I do not suppose I shall see Russia again." Then he told me he had sold all his milk for the *Endla*; but I let that pass, and he told me of how he had been a policeman in Hapsal – "a summer policeman," he explained, for in winter, it seems, there are no visitors, and policemen are not necessary – and how a man wearing a Cossack *bourka*, or long cloak, and talking very good Russian had told him that he had played cards with the Emperor. "It was clear enough that he was a great man." Then I put in another word about the milk, and he said something to his wife about milk for the *Endla*, and she laughed, and I guessed that the people of the *Endla* were going to get less perfect milk than they had hoped, for she took my milk-can and went off, while he told me there had been great rains, so that the water stood between the potato rows and the potatoes had rotted, and went on to ask if all was well with England. Then he noticed the eggs that I had bought at the inn. "Those are very little eggs," said he, and asked me what I had had to pay for them. I asked him if he had any, as we needed more for our ship, and he sent a little girl who brought ten beauties, twice the size of those already in my basket. Then the woman came back with my milk-can full of new milk warm from the cow, and he asked how he should know my little ship, so that his wife could bring me more milk in the morning, if we had not sailed. Then, when I paid for the eggs and the milk, he asked me if there was nothing else I wanted that he could give me, and I could think of nothing; but he gave me the best of his turnips and a lot of fresh beans, and with that he walked with me to an opening in the trees, whence we could see the harbour and *Racundra's* two masts. "If those masts are there in the morning," said he, "my wife shall bring you some more milk."

And so we parted, thanking each other, like old friends, and I hurried back by a quick way he showed me across country and came to the ship, and found that those hungry ones had finished supper and that my supper was cold, but I ate it with great pleasure, full of the warmth of this abundance of human intercourse.

"TOLEDO" OF LEITH

THE last time I was at Heltermaa was a year before we sailed in there in *Racundra*, when I came there on foot, after walking from the other side of the island, where I had landed from a small timber-carrying schooner in which I had sailed from the mainland. I came to Heltermaa by the road from Kerdla, and was hurrying back to rejoin the *Kittiwake* at Baltic Port. It so happened that I came there on a day when there were no means of getting across the Sound to Hapsal, and I was disconsolately trying to arrange with the innkeeper to let me sleep the night on a bench, when two sailors came in buying provisions. I tried them in my own language. One of them knew a few words, and told me that the captain of his ship spoke English, and that I had better come with them. I asked him where his ship was, and he pointed far out to sea, where, sure enough, a large steamship was lying.

I helped the men to carry a sack of potatoes, a tin of kerosene, milk, butter, bread and a lively little pig down to the tiny harbour. They had a small open boat, with a jib and spritsail, tied under the quay. We stowed everything into it, the pig squealing all the time with the regularity of a mechanical siren. We could not talk, but divided the labour in silent agreement. One man took the tiller, the other dealt with the sails, and I nursed the little pig. Within half an hour of my trudging into Heltermaa I was at sea, slipping rapidly over the four or five miles that separate Heltermaa from the Erik Stone.

As we came nearer, I was surprised at the way the ship was lying, broadside on to the wind and perfectly steady, across breaking waves. She was aground. Then, as we came nearer yet, I saw that her shrouds were dangling round the masts and

"TOLEDO" OF LEITH.

INHABITANTS OF MOON.

that she had been stripped bare. She was not, as I had supposed, a passing ship sending ashore for provisions. She was a wreck. I asked how long she had been there. "Two years or more. We are waiting for high water," said the man.

There was a rising wind, and we approached the wreck at great speed, shot round under her stern, luffed, lowered the sails and caught hold of a rope-ladder. As we came round under her stern I looked up for the name and read, "TOLEDO: LEITH". Here in this most unexpected of places was a British ship. I ran up the ladder and climbed over the bulwarks and down on the rusty shell of what once upon a time had steamed in all the pride of new paint and shining brasswork out of the Firth of Forth.

A small boy was hanging some fishing-nets to dry. He pointed aft when I asked for the captain, and, bending to avoid the nets and fishing-lines that were hanging under the upper deck, I groped my way towards the stern. Captain Konga, well over six feet high, came out of a sort of hutch he had rigged up between the decks. He greeted me in English, invited me into his cabin, told me I must stay the night with him, and promised to put me over to the mainland in the morning.

I have seen many cabins, but none quite like that hutch in which the captain of the *Toledo* had his comfortable being. It was built of baulks of wood set up on end between the iron decks. It was six feet six inches high, long and broad. That size, Captain Konga explained, he had found by experiment to be the most convenient. Sitting on his bunk, he could put wood on the stove in the corner, light his reading-lamp, take a book from the opposite shelf, eggs or bacon from his store-cupboard, reach down his saucepan or frying-pan from the hooks on the wall, or get the boatswain's whistle, with piercing blasts of which he summoned the members of his crew. From any place in it he could reach every other place, and that, he said, was the most labour saving kind of house.

He told me the story of the ship. She had been captured by the Germans in the summer of 1918. She had been aground on the shallows close by Heltermaa, but one wild night, while the Germans had all been drinking ashore, a strong westerly wind had so raised the waters in the Gulf that the *Toledo* floated off, and when the Germans came to look for her in the morning, she had floated far out to sea, and by miraculous chance had settled herself on this small shoal by the Erik Stone. The water had fallen again, and the Germans had lost the war and left these parts before it had ever again risen high enough to let them get her off. Then the Salvage Company had taken her over and Captain Konga had come to live on board. Once only in the previous winter, she had floated for a few minutes, but the ice round her was so thick that with the instruments at his command he could not shift her, and the sinking water had left her again in her place. Today the water was rising again. "Another four inches and we shall have her moving," said Captain Konga, and showed me the cables he had laid out astern, the little boiler and donkey-engine he had brought from Reval, and his other arrangements for pulling her into deep water the moment she should float. Actually, as we stood there, we could feel that she was on the point of floating. He had a marked pole over the side, and from time to time looked at it, to see if the water was still rising.

"Yet she isn't worth much, nowadays," he said. "The Germans stripped her of some things, and when they went the local pirates did the rest. They took everything, even pulling the engines to pieces to get the nuts. Nuts make good sinkers for fishing-nets. The portholes have all gone. All the new schooners built on Worms have fine brass portholes made in Edinburgh."

And here for two years Captain Konga had been living and enjoying himself most mightily. He shot seals which came and played by the rock. He painted the rock red. He shot duck. He fished. All passing boats took supplies of fresh fish from the *Toledo*. He made his own nets, and for his own amusement he kept his log, accurately as if at sea, but each day in a different language – Estonian, German, Swedish, English, Russian – ringing the changes on these five. He was delighted to talk English, and told me he had a friend in England, a very pretty young woman, living near Hull. He had taught her Russian and she had taught him English. "A very pretty young woman," said he. I asked him when he had last seen her, and he told me, twenty-five years ago. I hardly liked to suggest that the young woman might now be older, for he seemed so certain that for her at least time had stood still. "And so merry," he added, "and so active. Runs like a hare and dances . . . you should see her dance!"

Time, for Captain Konga, did not exist, except that he never had quite enough of it for all he wished to do. When I offered to send him newspapers, thinking foolishly that he might enjoy them, living alone out there on the wreck with Heltermaa as his metropolis, and that only approachable in fine weather in his little boat, he thanked me, but said he would never have time to read them, his life was so busy, what with birds, seals, fish, and the making of cartridges and nets and fishing-lines, drying, salting and skinning. He was enjoying himself enormously, and, as we talked, I perceived that he always had enjoyed himself enormously, looking neither before nor after, but whole-heartedly engaged in whatsoever he was doing. And he had done strange things, hunting bears in the Arctic, hunted himself by the women of the Samoyeds maddened by the drinks of civilization. He had his whole life at his fingers' ends. It was all contemporaneous for him, and talking of this or that, as he taught me how to make a net, he would refer to events of thirty years ago as if they had happened that same afternoon.

Next day it blew so hard that it was almost impossible to stand on deck, except in the shelter of the bulwarks, so I spent another night with Captain Konga, netting, and hearing tales of the Esthonian coast, of Ungern Sternberg and his wreckers, of the people of the Tutters islands, who will not let the Salvage Company approach a wreck before the men of Tutters have finished with it. "The sea was black with their little boats, and as I came near with a tug, they shouted at me to keep off, and waved every man a gun to show that they were armed." "But that was a long time ago," said I. "It was last year, or the year before. These people do not change so fast. I've had to show that we have guns to keep them off the *Toledo*. The Dagö folk are quiet enough, but the men of Worms . . . and the men of Worms are sucking babes beside the pirates of Tutters."

On the second morning the sea was going down and the wind was less, and the captain and one of his men lowered away the little skiff that he had for fishing. There was just room for the three of us in her. We sailed due E. to the island of Worms, thinking that I should there catch the postman's cutter for Hapsal. We came upon patches of rocks, awash and out of the water. Then the man lowered the sprit, reducing the sail by one-half as we threaded our way among them. Now and again we were skimming over less than a foot of water. Once we stepped out and carried the boat over a shallower place. Then out in deep water again, and the little boat, which was Captain Konga's special pride, fairly slipped across the waves. We landed on the eastern corner of Worms by Sviby, but the post cutter had gone, and the captain looked at his watch. It was just possible that we might catch the train at Hapsal. We were off again, but as Hapsal came in sight saw the train steaming in the station. It is nearly two miles from the pier to the station. The thing could not be done. "How many minutes have we?" asked the captain. I told him. He said nothing, but turned aside from the fairway leading to the pier and steered straight across the rocky shoals at the station. We touched once, again, and sat every moment expecting to ground for good. But luck was with us, as it must always be with such as Captain Konga, and with two minutes to spare he ran the boat ashore and I jumped for the train.

That autumn the water gave him his chance and he took it, pulled the *Toledo* off, and with the help of a tug from Reval took her to Helsingfors. I felt sorry for him when I heard it. As a salved ship, in these days, I do not suppose the *Toledo* was worth much, nor would his share of that be large. But as a fishing and shooting box, for a man like him, who knew how to use every moment of his time in such pursuits, she was without a better in the world.

FROM THE ISLAND OF DAGÖ TO THE ISLAND OF MOON

AT Heltermaa we were to stay for longer than we wished. We lay there from the 12th to the 17th of September, watching the barometer and the sky and getting sharp pains in the backs of our necks from looking up the mast at the wimpel, which for all that time showed us a wind in our teeth, while, as we could see from the bowing spar-buoys outside, there was a current to match it. To beat S. against wind and stream was hopeless. So we lay there and talked of how when our own wind came we would fly southward through the Moon Sound and then run from end to end of the Riga Gulf in a single twenty-four hours. When our wind came we actually did that run in many hours less, and most of it under almost bare poles, but our wind was a long time in coming. Meanwhile there was plenty of wind of the wrong sort, which blew our flag to pieces and unravelled it until there was hardly any of it left. The Ancient made a new long wimpel from a strip of red bunting, and when I joked with him for hoisting a Bolshevik flag, replied: "It'll give the wind a fright and make it blow the other way." But the wind seemed rather to relish it, and blew on day after day.

The second day after our arrival there was half a gale from the S.E., and a heavy swell came through the wooden piles of the pier. The schooner from Worms had warped into the quay to load apples and we had shifted to make room, and then tied up to the schooner, hoping for better protection. But that night, at two o'clock in the morning, a loud crack brought me on deck, barefoot and in pyjamas, to meet the Ancient, who had tumbled up out of the forehatch at the same moment, and the two of us, just in time, hanging on a rope with all the strength we had, held

A HOUSE ON MOON.

A HOUSE ON MOON TODAY.

Racundra, while we fixed a new warp to replace the stout one that had parted. It had chafed through in spite of heavy parcelling, and thereafter we not only served and parcelled it where it crossed the schooner's railing, but spliced it as if it were a broken limb, binding chips of firewood round it, so that it lay snug in a wooden shell. Even that had worn thin before we left, but the rope was kept in perfect condition, and the dodge is one to recommend to any other little cruisers in such circumstances.

Not all the inhabitants of Dagö were as friendly to us as those with whom I had talked on that first evening. Some are stern patriots, and show their feelings by refusing to talk the languages which, until in 1919 they became independent, had been imposed on them by force. All three of us knew a few words of Esthonian and made what play we could with them, but when it came to serious business had to use Russian, German or Swedish. Now, there was one stout old man in top-boots who used to come down on the quay and seemed to have authority among the others. He had said "Good-day" to us in Esthonian once, and we had replied in Esthonian, for politeness' sake, and perhaps from pride in this small scrap of our uncertain vocabulary. But next day, when he came again, the Ancient, talking Russian, tried to learn from him where he could buy meat, and the Esthonian flushed red and angry, and asked him what he was talking Russian for, when he had shown the day before that he could talk Esthonian as well as himself. The poor Ancient tried to make him believe that he knew how to say "Good-morning", but did not know how to say anything else, but the Esthonian would not be appeased, turned his back on him and took up a fine Napoleon attitude on the pierhead, "as if," said the Ancient, "he would like to be the stone figure of a patriot." Unfortunately, however, he was not content with being a stone figure, but tried to persuade others of his fellow-countrymen to have no dealings with us except in Esthonian. After that there were two factions among the people who came down to the quay – the patriots who would have nothing to do with us and the cosmopolitans who sold us what they had and made us presents of ripe apples and worms for our fishing, and, when in the middle of the night the little steamer came from

Reval, woke us up with shouts from the quay, lest we should miss our share of the general happy excitement. The two factions came often to hot words, and among the younger members to blows; and we, who had hoped in *Racundra* to escape politics of any kind, found it a little tedious to be bones of contention. We felt, in our little ship in that foreign harbour, what a small nation must feel while its fate is being discussed by greater Powers.

During the days when we were not fishing, and, since the wind from the south was blowing the bait in the fishes' mouth, catching plenty of good fish suppers, we walked on the island. We found a great number of fossils on the beach – stone sponges and petrified shells of different shapes. We also found lucky stones, with natural holes in them, like (but how different from!) the lucky stone on *Racundra's* cabin wall, that came from Coniston and the friendliest house in England. It was warm in the sunshine, and I saw a green woodpecker, but he is with us all the year, and from other signs it was only too clear that winter was falling swiftly upon us. The starlings were in great flocks. The leaves on the trees were turning and the nights were growing long. The very apples that were being brought down to the quay in little springless carts and carefully packed away in the hold of the schooner beside us were a warning that the days were coming when, in these waters at any rate, little ships cannot keep the sea. The Ancient began talking with persistent gloom about "the Equinotion time", when the Gulf of Riga would be at its very worst. The autumn equinox of September 23rd was indeed close at hand; and we were held here as if by some malice of its own to wait for its notorious inhospitality.

However, when we had begun to think that we should have to run back to Reval, lay the yacht up there and get back to work, we were released in cat-and-mouse fashion and allowed to get a little farther S. Late in the night of September 16th there was a breath of wind from the W. We hardly dared to trust it, but, with faint hope, set alarm-clocks to wake us early. At half-past six next morning the wind freshened from the W. again, and ten minutes later we were swinging from the end of the pier on a single warp while we hoisted sail. Five minutes after that, with main and mizen set, we cast off, rejoicing like prisoners released, and running up our staysail when we were already under way. By half-past seven we were well out into the Sound, and bore up on the starboard tack to pass about a mile E. of the island of Heinlaid. Thence we steered S. by E. and ³/₄E., looking for the bell-buoy in the middle of the Sound.

The wind was one to stir the blood and we were all in the best of spirits, taking it in turns to go below and eat great quantities of porridge, when we sighted a biggish steamer coming up from the S., with buff funnel and black top to it, and the peculiar bows that belong to our friend the *Baltabor*. As she came nearer, however, the Ancient, whose eyes are usually better than mine, decided that she was not the *Baltabor* but a German. "Yet her bows are awfully like," I said, "though she has hardly had time to go to England and back since she steamed out of Reval harbour with the Pelorus she had promised to lend us still on board." These words I said as I turned to go below, but I was not half-way down the companion steps when I was stopped by the *Baltabor's* siren. I had gone down for the strong binoculars, but did not need them now. Yes; the *Baltabor* it was, and . . .quick with that ensign. . . . Whalley has sent a man to the jack staff. Up goes our ensign, flutters at the mizen top, dips half-way down and up again, while our big friend's ensign, about as broad as our mainsail, does the same. It was the very pleasantest of greetings between the big and little British ships meeting each other on this cold, sunny September morning on a sea so utterly unlike the seas of England. Moreover, we were doing 5.6 knots at the time, and that was a mighty satisfaction, as the last occasion on which *Baltabor* had seen us under sail was when we were slowly tacking through the Mühlgraben by Riga, and we were afraid she might have been given a poorish notion of our speed.

We sighted our bell-buoy close on the port bow, just where it should have been, and this, together with *Baltabor* and the sun and the blue water and the keen air and the wind that suited *Racundra* from truck to keel, all combined to make us delighted with ourselves and Fate. But we patted Fate on the back too soon. "We shall be in Riga tomorrow," we cried, as we saluted

THE GATES OF MOON.

THE GATES OF MOON TODAY.

the bell-buoy triumphantly, and steered southwards to bring the beacons of the island of Moon in a line. But, just as we did so, we found we were standing nearly close-hauled. The wind was backing to the S. again. We were now retracing the course we had followed when running up from Paternoster on the outward voyage, and at 10.45 passed the Moon light-buoy, finished with the Moon beacons and steered for those of Shildau Island. An hour later we were past Shildau, and at noon, the wind having gone definitely to S.W. and strengthened very much, were steering for the Kuivast anchorage, to bring up there and see what was going to happen next. The aged cutter that plies as ferry-boat between Kuivast and the mainland passed on the port tack close across our bows and then went about. We raced them for the anchorage and beat them, anchoring at 12.30 close off the pier at Kuivast in two fathoms, stiff clay bottom, and getting our sails down in time to watch the cutter bring up to the pier. Here were a number of cattle awaiting it, and we saw for the first time the fiery orange petticoats and black bodices which are the national costume of the women of Moon. We watched the women go on board with their cattle, and then, as it was clear that we were in for another southerly storm, put the covers on the sails. We had made good something over twenty-five miles.

There is no harbour at Kuivast, nothing but a short pier, crooked at the outer end, but enclosing so small a space that even the little steamers never attempt to enter it. The ferry-cutter tied up inside to load cattle, but had only just room, the rest of the space being occupied by two small waterlogged barges. The anchorage immediately off the pier is very good, as far as holding-capacity goes, but very bad as regards protection. We learnt later that we had dropped our anchor in the best possible place, as farther south the rock is very near the surface. Indeed, a schooner that anchored there dragged her hook and had to spend the night beating. The protection is even worse than appears, as we were to learn to our cost. On the chart the place would seem to be perfectly sheltered from all winds between S.W. and N.W. This is not so. With both southerly and northerly winds, owing perhaps to some trick of the variable current, the swell rushes across the wind and breaks over the Kuivast pier.

Both English and German charts mark this place as the best anchorage. For smaller vessels, however, there is now a very much better stopping-place on the other side of the Sound. Of that, however, we knew nothing when we arrived.

The orange-petticoated women drove their cattle into the cutter, and for some time a few of the men of Moon watched us from the pierhead, but presently, as it began to blow harder, men and women alike went off to the shelter of the tumble-down houses. It was not till late in the afternoon, when the wind slackened, that the cutter thought fit to sail, when it made straight across the Sound to some landing-place on the other side. Then, not wishing to lose the chance of saying that I had at least talked with some of the people of Moon, I made up my mind to go ashore. The Ancient helped me to sling the dinghy overboard with the fore-halyard, and I tumbled in with the milk-can and pulled for the landing place.

Under the wall of a half-ruined cottage close to the shore was a bench, and on it were four of the men of Moon, or rather, three men of Moon and a policeman in a neat grey uniform, who told me that he, too, was a foreigner in this place, since he had not been born on Moon, but on the larger island of Oesel. I greeted them with "Tere, tere" as I approached, and was answered in the same way. Then I tried English on the policeman. He knew what it was, though he could not speak it, and I heard him announce his discovery to the others. Then I tried Russian and found he could talk Russian just about as badly as I talk it myself. The others knew only two or three words of the language, but, unlike the patriots of Heltermaa, they were willing enough to use the words they knew, and, indeed, put them eagerly, by way of punctuation marks, into the conversation between the policeman and myself.

The policeman was a delightful fellow: asked where we were going, praised the speed of our little ship as compared with that of the ferry-cutter, told me not to use the water from the well by the pier, because it and everything cooked with it would taste of seaweed, but to take water from the other well by the inn. "At least," he said, lest he should raise false hopes, "it used to be an inn." When I asked for milk, he volunteered at once to take me to this ci-devant tavern, and, in case the man there or his wife did not understand to translate for me. With that we sauntered up the muddy lane together and passed without ceremony through the stone Gates of Moon.

From *Racundra's* deck I had seen these two strange stone columns on either side of the road leading inland from the pier and had asked the Ancient what he made of them.

"Those," said he, "mighta be the Gates of Moon, of which I have often heard tell. The barons that lived here did all for themselves as themselves liked best, and would allow no one to land on Moon without he went through those gates, and no one through those gates without he paid what the barons thought they could get from him." This sounded a little too much like Huck Finn's account of kings, so I had gone ashore with an open mind.

I asked the policeman what the pillars were.

"There are a lot of fairy tales about them," said he, "but I think myself that they were set up in honour of the Emperor Nicholas 1 when he visited the island of Moon."

That explanation at least was one of the fairy tales. The Ancient had been nearer the mark. Beside the pillars I now noticed a stone cross. Cross and pillars alike seemed to be of about the same age, something near 1600, I should think, but fixed on one of the pillars was a stone placard of later date, perhaps eighteenth or early nineteenth century. This placard was in German and Russian and set out a tariff of tolls – so much for a carriage, so much for a cart, so much for a peasant's cart, so much for a cow, so much for a peasant's cow, so much for a man, and, finally, so much for a dog. There must have been some lively incidents in the attempted collection of tolls from sportive, energetic dogs, who might run in and out ten times in as many minutes while the toll-keeper was dealing with larger folk. The actual sums demanded had been obliterated. On the other pillar, opposite the tariff, was a coat-of-arms, I believe that of the old German castle town of Arensburg, a fat and bloated bird with upstretched neck, standing on two straight legs. No. It was clear enough that the Ancient's story was nearer the truth and that the gates are the last memorials of the German rulers of

THE OLD RUSSIAN INN AT KUIVAST.

RUSSIAN INN AT KUIVAST TODAY.

Moon, who transferred their allegiance from Sweden to Russia on finding that the Russian Empire left them a freer hand in exploiting the Esthonians than was given them by the more liberal-minded Swedes.

The Gates were the last symbol of the German civilization. The inn was the last symbol of the Russian. It was a typical Russian posting-station, a low, one-storied building, with pillars along the front of it, where, as throughout Russia only seven crowded years ago, it was possible to get bad food and good horses and a night's lodging, the quality of which depended on the thickness of your skin. The Russian stoves were still there. So were the great beds, where from a dozen to twenty people could sleep together on straw or hay. The little counter, where the Imperial vodka was once sold, remained. But there were no horses, no vodka, no sleepers – nothing, in fact, of former glory. The innkeeper, who seemed to be also harbour-master, told me that he had once had some beer, but that there was none left. Once upon a time, he said, he had had some local kvas. Now he had nothing except . . . he pointed to a few packets of cigarettes. He had no tobacco. The policeman and I drank a couple of glasses of clear cold water, handed by the innkeeper over the counter where so many gallons of vodka had passed in days gone by. He then showed me the well, the only one, as both innkeeper and policeman enthusiastically agreed, where the water is fit for humans. And meanwhile the innkeeper's daughter, a young woman whose round, flat jolly face might well be placed on the Gates of Moon as the emblem of her island, instead of that toll-fattened bird, went off and milked a cow, and gave me my can full of admirable milk, two quarts of it, for some Esthonian marks, the value of which in English money would be about fourpence. With this I returned to the ship.

KUIVAST TO WERDER

I had a hard job not to spill the milk as I pulled back to *Racundra*. The wind was piping up again from the S.W. and the swell of which I have already spoken was beginning to come in. *Racundra* was jerking about in so lively a manner that I decided to put out our larger anchor (sixty-seven pounds) and the stout coir cable. The Ancient and I, hauling together, had as much as we could do in pulling the ship up towards the first anchor. We did this with the tiller lashed over, giving her something of a sheer, so that we should not be dropping the second anchor on the chain. We then let go and veered out fifteen fathoms or more of cable and chain. We lay in two fathoms, ample, for we draw only a little over half a fathom with our centreboard up. We then had supper and turned in.

But we got little rest that night. The wind increased to a gale, and, sheltered though we were, the current kept *Racundra* across both wind and swell, with the result that she rolled me out of my bunk on the top of the big iron pump that was stowed on the floor, sent things adrift that we had considered fast till doomsday, including a water-cask, fortunately empty, and used every loose thing in the ship to make a noise like a negro band. It was impossible to sleep. All that could be done was to sit on the bunks, wedge one's knees firmly against the centreboard-case and count how many rolls *Racundra* could accomplish in a minute. Again and again the Ancient and I crawled over the deck to see if we were dragging. We took the covers off again, and had everything ready to make sail in a moment, but did not wish to do so unless obliged, as we did not then know where to seek shelter without going right back to Heltermaa. *Racundra* rolled until she took water on her decks over the railings, in spite of her notable freeboard. But the anchors held and morning found us still desperately rolling, in a swell that was splashing over the pier and made us glad that we had, according to our custom, taken the dinghy inboard for the night. It was too rough to launch the little boat again. The motion was such that we could not cook, nor even make tea. So we lived on cold bacon, tinned herrings and beer, and relieved our feelings by punching the barometer.

In the afternoon there was less wind. The barometer had fallen to 29.2, but now showed just the faintest inclination to rise, and at four o'clock, as there were patches of sunshine, I went ashore and took photographs, though it was still blowing in gusts that made it very hard to keep the camera steady. An hour later, however, the wind dropped suddenly, and the Ancient and I shouldered water-tank and barrel and went half a mile inland for the water that was fit for humans, as we began to hope that we should be off for Riga in the morning. I further took the opportunity of asking where the cutter lay at the other side of the Sound. She had not reappeared, so I was sure that she had on the other side a better shelter than was to be found here. I learnt that during the war a new harbour had been built at Werder, of which all my charts were ignorant. I got rough sailing directions. "Steer straight across for the southernmost of three white ruined houses, and when you come near you will see the harbour and can go into it. There are twelve feet of water, and tugs have wintered there."

This sounded promising, so when in the morning, after a rather better night, we found a bright day, but with wind and strong current still against us from the S., I had the sails up soon after breakfast and we went across the Sound in plenty of time to come back if we should be disappointed in what we should find there. The cutter, held up yesterday by the bad weather, had returned to Kuivast, taken on board more red cattle and orange petticoats, and set sail on her way back just after we started. There was enough wind, however, to make *Racundra* a fast boat, and we had the wind on our beam, so

THE NEW HARBOUR AT WERDER.

THE HARBOUR AT WERDER TODAY.

we kept them well astern until we had gone far enough to see a decent-looking harbour with a schooner's masts above it, but nothing to show on which side was the entry. When I can use local knowledge, I always prefer it to my own ignorance, so, much to the cutter's astonishment, I brought *Racundra* to the wind, hove her to, and waited for them to catch us. But such was the modesty of the cutter's crew that they never guessed why we were waiting, and themselves hauled up to the wind and proceeded extremely slowly, as if they thought we had perceived some special danger ahead. They stared with all their eyes. At last, however, they went on, and giving them a fair start, we let the staysail draw and proceeded after them. Just as we did so, the wind, which had been moderate, strengthened with a sudden squall, so that cutter and *Racundra* alike fairly foamed across the remaining distance. We saw that the cutter steered to northwards of the harbour mole, so we did the same, and a minute or two later, had rounded into as fine a little harbour for small ships as ever I hope to see. We anchored and then, deciding to stay, ran a warp out to the pier and berthed ourselves under the shelter of a huge stack of birch logs, which, since they were much weathered, I concluded had been there some time and were not likely to fly about our heads.

We had found this harbour of Werder, or Wirtsu, as the Esthonians call it, just in time. That night the wind came from the N.W. with rain and such violence that the waves breaking on the mole flung great bits of themselves not only over the mole but clean over the woodpile, fifteen feet across and as many high, and down with heavy splashes on *Racundra's* cabin roof on the other side. A big open cutter, rather like the ferryboat, lying beside us was half filled during the night by the water tossed across the mole. At six in the morning the wind was blowing from the N. with similar force, but swung round to S. again at eleven, giving us a comparatively calm afternoon and evening.

I spent the better part of that day fishing on the sheltered side of the pier, and caught upwards of fifty little fish – *killos*, boneless little creatures like sardines, extremely good to eat.

THE NEW LIGHTHOUSE AT WERDER BESIDE THE FOUNDATIONS OF
THE OLD LIGHTHOUSE, WHICH WAS BLOWN UP DURING THE WAR.

WERDER LIGHTHOUSE TODAY.

I also had a pleasant talk with an elderly Robinson Crusoe, master and owner of a little open boat, smaller even than *Racundra*, who was doing his best to get his things dry after the tempestuous night. He had spent the summer carrying stones at Reval, and now was sailing home for the winter in his own little boat to a bay some half a dozen miles south of Werder. His boat was filled with all manner of treasure acquired during the summer – bits of old iron, empty bottles, a lump or two of good oak, salt, tobacco and other valuables. The salt and such things he stowed in a cuddy forward. He slept under his sails and cooked on a little open stove in the stern. He was plucking a duck for his dinner when I got into talk with him. He had shot it the day before, while sheltering behind a little rocky island farther north. He showed me his gun, a fowling-piece that might have been the envy of Man Friday. He knew a little English, having sailed three years on English ships. He also knew Lettish, a rare accomplishment among Esthonians, in whose folklore devils talk Lettish to each other, which is also the language spoken in hell. He had travelled enough to lose such national prejudices, and sat there, plucking and cooking his duck, talking with obvious pride with the Ancient and me, with each in his own language. In the calm of the evening he put to sea, and the last we saw of him was the dark blot of his sail as he rowed and poled his boat over the shallows and into the Gulf, in this way avoiding the current. At night, when the storm rose again, with fierce rain-squalls, we feared for him, but there was no need. He knew the coast, as he had told us, like the palm of his hand; and the lighthouse-keeper, who visited us in the morning, told us that he had seen the little boat both at dusk and dawn, and that our friend had spent the night snugly in smooth water behind some rocks, with white waves on every hand.

The next day the wind was from the S.W. and for the next five days swung to and fro, blowing nearly all the time with tremendous force. For all that time the ferry cutter was unable to cross from Werder to Kuivast. Peasants from Werder and the mainland and men of Moon and their orange-skirted dames came to the harbour and day after day hung desolately about the cutter in wind and rain, at night getting what shelter they could in the forest. "This 'is' the Equinotion time," said the Ancient philosophically, "and this is what musta be." He, however, could afford to be philosophic, for he had made his berth tight and comparatively dry, and so was much better off than the unfortunate islanders waiting in the woods for the ferry to take them home.

It was a wild time. Late one evening we watched a big schooner, close-hauled, trying to make the entrance of the Sound from the south. (This was during a north-wester.) As she came she pointed nearer the wind and made less and less headway, and it became clear that she could not make the entrance without tacking. They hung on till the last minute and then tried to go about. She would not stay. Again and again the sails flapped and filled again, while the schooner lost ground. Finally, with jibs wildly flogging, she let go her anchor. Down came the sails one after another, and we watched her heaving half her length out of the water, dipping her nose under and rearing again. The anchor held for ten minutes. Then, not slowly as with dragging anchor, but in a sudden rush, with parted cable, she was swept away southwards behind the point, broadside on, a helpless thing, just as dark fell. What became of her I do not know. The lighthouse-keeper told us that she did not go on the rocks, but was swept clear of them to the south. He saw no attempt made to hoist sail. "They were tired out," he said, "tired beyond work, and seeing they were drifting clear, perhaps made up their minds to let her drift till forty miles south, when they would maybe be rested and have a chance of getting into shelter in the Pernau bight."

During that same blow, another schooner under jib and reefed foresail, coming from the north, swept at terrific speed into our harbour, let go her anchor without standing upon the order of its going, far too near the shore, and, while it dragged, rowed desperately in their small boat and made fast a warp to the pier with perhaps ten seconds to spare in saving her. The men from the other schooner that had been there when we arrived jumped to lend a hand, and she was presently berthed alongside the quay. The men of this schooner had brought with them a mixed cargo from the town of Reval, salt fish, kerosene and farming-tools; and during the next two days the people of the country brought them in exchange corn in sacks, four or five sacks stuffed into each rickety little springless cart. They also brought them a fine sheep, which was killed and skinned on the quay and its flesh then cut up, weighed, paid for and put into a barrel with salt, provision for their voyage. They were taking the corn to Petrograd. The other schooner here was loading firewood for Reval.

There was nothing to be done with the weather, for though now and again the wind veered northwards it always backed swiftly to the S.W., while the sea remained in frothy tumult. It was as if the Equinox had amused himself by setting N.W. and S.W. to fight each other, and now one and now the other got the mastery in a struggle the tension of which hardly slackened for a moment. I made a curve of our barometer readings on squared paper during that week, but it might have been taken for a graphic record of the progress of a grasshopper. When we came to Werder the barometer was at 29.28. After that it bobbed up and down between 29 and 29.55. It had been 29.9 when we left Hapsal to get into this bout of bad weather. Often it was nearly impossible to stand on the quay, and we were thankful for our woodpile, behind which was comparative peace. There was no village nearer than six miles away, and we ran out of eggs, meat, potatoes, bread and, worst of all, tobacco. The few houses by the old pier that was used before the building of the harbour are in ruins, and we should have been in a very bad way if it had not been for the keeper of the Werder Lighthouse, which, by the way, is not in the least like the picture of it still reproduced on the English charts, but is a plain wooden framework replacing the old tower, which was blown up during the war. The lighthouse-keeper lives with his wife and three children in a wooden shanty close by, on a desolate spit of bare ground running out from the woods into the sea. He used to come and sit in the cabin of *Racundra* and I used to visit him in

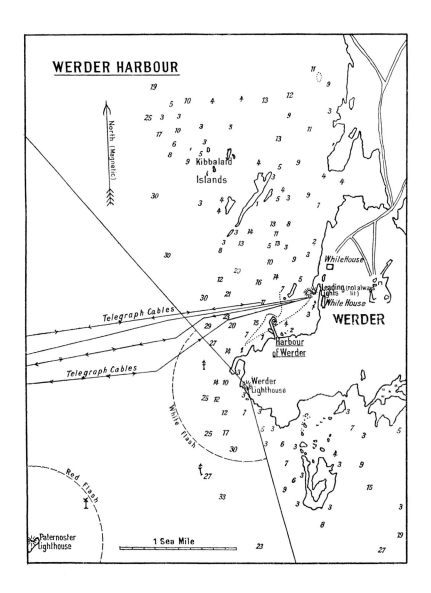

CHART OF WERDER HARBOUR.

his shanty. The only blemish on his conversation was that, like his brother of Runö, similarly isolated from the world, he took an interest in politics, and wanted to know what we were doing about Egypt. However, he made up for that by selling us milk, butter and potatoes, and he also gave me some tobacco of his own growing, raw leaves not yet dry, which I hung over the cabin lamp till they crackled, and then broke them up and smoked them, and found them a very great deal better than no tobacco at all.

Our most interesting visitors, however, were two seal-hunters from Runö. I saw them buffeting their way along the quay afar off, and knew at once what they must be. No other men wear pale homespuns bound with black and hairy sealskin shoes. No other men go abroad with long telescopes and crooked sticks. No other men on reaching our woodpile would climb upon the top of it, crouching low against the wind, and, steadying the end of the telescope by using the stick as a support, would search so patiently the distant rocks. Presently they were close to us, and stood there, one young man, one elderly, looking down at *Racundra* from the quay with eyes so simple that you would think they had never been troubled by a thought. The Ancient talked with them and told me that they begged . . . for what? For glass bottles, the one thing they do not make upon their island. They needed bottles for oil, for carrying water, for what not? We gave them a lot of empty beer-bottles. They took off their caps and shook our hands. Then they asked if they might come on board. They came and went down into the cabin, fingering everything, enormously, inarticulately interested.

"A strong ship," said the younger, at last. "We too have a strong ship, with five little ones which she carries inside her."

"And where is your ship?"

"Over there, a half-hour's walk, in a better harbour than this."

"And are there five of you?"

"Yes, five. Three we left on an island off the coast of Oesel, with their three boats. We are now two. In four weeks we shall sail back along the Oesel coast and find our men, and then we go to Runö again."

"Have you got many seals?"

"Only one. The weather is too bad for them, but later we shall have more."

There was a little more simple question and answer of this kind. Then they saw my camera and asked what it was. I told them, and the younger one understood at once, and said that they had seen photographs that had been taken on Runö by some Swedish visitor, who had afterwards sent them to the island. They were delighted when I suggested making a picture of their ship. They wanted me to come at once, but I told them that for picture-making I needed a good light, and not a raging storm with wind and hail. If it should clear later I would come. With that we all gravely shook hands and they went off.

SEAL HUNTERS FROM RUNÖ

SEPTMEBER 24th. Last night we had a further taste of the Equinox in a northerly gale with heavy rain. This morning, however, though the wind continued, the sky cleared, the sun shone, and I made up my mind to sail this evening, if the weather held and the barometer, now slowly rising, did not take another dive. In the meantime I determined to use Sunday morning by repaying the visit of the men of Runö. I had promised to photograph their ship.

I saw the men of Runö about a mile away on shore, conspicuous in their pale homespuns, and, slinging my camera on my back, was blown along the pier and almost off it as I hurried in pursuit of them. "These men live on a little island," said I to myself, "therefore they cannot be good walkers. At any rate I, who have spent half my life afoot on the fells of England, ought to be able to catch up with them." Catch them I did, but after a long struggle, though they did not seem to be hurrying. The older, shorter man was using his carved stick as a staff, the younger was turning in his toes as he walked, and yet they kept up a steady pace, as regular as animals. Trotting beside them was a boy, whose dress proclaimed him of the mainland. The men of Runö were, I think, wandering round on this Sunday morning to see what they could gather from the people of the continent. When at last I caught them, they had stopped at one of the few inhabited cottages, and the young one, after greeting me with joy and agreeing at once to take me to their ship, bitterly complained that the house was shut up and no one was at home. He pointed to the sun and to my camera case, remembering that I had told him yesterday that I could photograph his ship only if there was a good sun.

SEAL HUNTERS, THEIR BOAT AND SHIP.

THE SEAL HUNTERS ON BOARD THEIR SHIP.
(Note the flint-lock gun.)

We set off across country, the men of Runö swearing that it was not far to the ship. We passed through the grounds of a ruined country house, a fine place before the war, but now a desolate shell; then out over wide marshland, and, after half an hour's walking, they pointed to a white mast against the shadow of a distant wood. The men of Runö and I walked our natural pace, and the Esthonian boy trotted at our heels. As we walked we talked, a sort of Volapuk or Esperanto, composed of German, Swedish and Russian words stirred well together with a lot of goodwill. We understood one another excellently. They explained that the rig of their boat was not like that of the Esthonians, but was a traditional rig from older times than man can remember, and peculiar to Runö. They told me that they had a fine gun, that there were pike in some water to the left of us, that they had shot good duck in a bight on the other side, and so on. I told them that we were sailing in the evening, but they both vehemently protested. "No, no! It will blow again a great storm in the night, but in the morning will be clear weather and a fair wind for Riga." I pointed to the clear blue sky overhead, but they would have none of it. "Man fran Runö kens wetter. Bettra i morgen. Clockan fem segel. En gud wind till Riga," and so on, with such insistence that I made up my mind to wait till morning and see if the men of Runö knew the weather as well as they thought they did.

Talking so, we came through a little wood to a tiny natural harbour, where their ship lay at anchor, a strange ship indeed, bigger than *Racundra*, but not much, with a long bowsprit, a foremast with a high spritsail, and a mainmast of great length, exactly in the middle of the ship, with a marked rake towards the stern, a short gaff and a very long boom projecting far over the counter. Drawn up on the grassy shore were two little boats shaped like narrow spoons, that could, I should think, be used either with oars or with a single paddle like a canoe. I took a photograph of the ship as she lay there, with the little boats on the shore, and each man ran of his own accord to be photographed each by his own little boat, which, as they explained, each had made for himself. The Esthonian boy wanted to be photographed also, but they would have none of this and drove him away, saying that he was not from Runö and therefore should not be in the picture. He ran off angrily into the woods, and we saw him no more. Then we all three got into one of the little boats, and the younger man ferried us out to the ship. I sat in the stern, the younger man rowed in the bows, and the elder squatted in the bottom by way of ballast. The ship had her name in blue and white elaborately painted on her counter: "JUBA: RUNÖ". They brought the boat stern foremost under the counter and I scrambled up and in.

Whatever the *Juba* might want in cleanliness, and she wanted a good deal, she made up in strength. She was built in 1911 on Runö. The elder man had taken part in the building. Her planking was of oak, two inches thick, I judged, and her ribs – square-sided ribs of ash or elm, I could not be certain from their description which they meant – were enormously heavy. The counter was partially decked, the whole of the midships portion was open, while the forepart of the ship was decked over with a high curved roof, making a very roomy forecastle. In front of the mainmast were two big barrels, one full of seal-fat, the other of seal-flesh. A skin was drying in the sun. In the covered forecastle, a great space, bigger even than *Racundra's* prided cabin, were stowed a great mass of sails and all kinds of gear. They burrow under the sails to sleep. There were shelves along the sides with rough wooden spoons and boxes which they decorate with fire, scraps of leather, partly made shoes, hanks of yarn and fishing-tackle. They brought out their seal-gun, a muzzle-loading flintlock that might have been used by the Jacobites. They had made a case for it of sealskin with the hair outside. The elder man had also a Japanese rifle, but they both agreed that the ancient flint was "bettra". I asked them if they were going to sell the sealskin in Arensburg. "No," they said; "the sealskins are wanted for the making of shoes for the people of Runö." They showed me their own furry shoes, with up-pointed tips and worked leather borders, very fine shoes indeed, for this was Sunday, and just as today they were wearing the newest of pale homespun jackets, with trousers like straight tubes to match, so they were wearing new shoes, both shoes and clothes being identical with those they had worn yesterday except for their newness. Everything they wore they had made themselves on the island or in their ship, with the exception of their caps. The elder had a cap of plain blue, the younger a Newmarket check cloth cap, faded almost white, with holes through which shreds of pink silk lining showed, but still a fine thing from foreign parts and worn with Sunday clothes in simple pride.

They told me they came every year to this particular little inlet. I asked how many years – twenty? Far more. The older man said that his father had brought him there the first time he came. I have no doubt that for not ten or twenty but for several hundred years a little ship of strange rig has anchored there and emptied out of its hold the little spoon-shaped sealing boats, and simple men in pale clothes bound with black, with ornamental shoes of sealskin. These men, perhaps better than any other Europeans except the Laplanders, continue into our times the life their forebears lived in the Middle Ages and earlier. Steam has meant nothing to them except a visit from a steamboat once a year. The Iron Age brought them knives and iron boat-fastenings (though even now they often build without). A flintlock gun, a Japanese rifle, that rare treasure of a Newmarket cap: what are these but trifles? They could kill seals and cover their heads without these things. One thing of real value to them dropped from civilization they had indeed upon the *Juba*, and they brought it to me in its box and opened its dark magic with proper reverence. It was an old dry compass from a maker in Wapping, taken, no doubt, from some ship wrecked fifty years ago on the rocky western shores of their island.

We parted with high mutual esteem, expressed by an exchange. I gave them the old pipe I was smoking. The elder man gave me a worn tobacco-pouch. "Fran England till Runö. Fran Runö till England," he said, carefully stowing my pipe upon his crowded shelf. Then there was tremendous handshaking and bowing and taking off of caps. After which the younger man took me ashore. I had got his name, and he begged me to send him the pictures, addressed simply "Arensburg for Runö." "We shall get them next summer when the steamer comes".

WERDER TO RIGA

THE men of Runö were so far right that it blew hard during the night, though the storm they had expected was reserved for us on the night after. In the morning of September 25th, at eight o'clock, the barometer was at 29.4, and at ten was half a point higher. For the first time for a fortnight it had been for forty-eight hours comparatively steady, and not on the upward or downward grade of a steep switchback. The wind was N.W. The little Russian steamer which, going south like ourselves, had waited by Kuivast all the previous day was getting her anchor. I had a feeling that now was our chance, and that we had better take it before, as it were, the Equinox got his second wind.

"What about sailing?" said I to the Ancient, who was on the pier sheltering behind the woodpile and looking through the glasses at the little steamer.

"We can but try," said he.

And with that we began casting off the spider's web of stout warps with which we had been keeping *Racundra* quiet during the last five days of mixed gales. Ten minutes later she was swinging to her anchor. Ten minutes after that we had the sails up and everything lashed down on deck and made snug below, and at 10.45 we had got our anchor and were beating out into the Sound under bright sunshine and a blue sky with racing clouds, the outlines of which encouraged us by being very much softer than the oily, knife-edged affairs of the last few days. At a quarter past eleven we were close to the mouth of the Sound. Paternoster Lighthouse on Virelaid Island, a compact little hummock with rocks all round it and rock-like haystacks on the low land behind it, bore W. by S. We were level with the second Werder buoy, the open sea was before us, and I set our course due S., which should give us a sight of Runö Lighthouse to help us in the night. *Racundra* was going a grand pace, and our faith in the men of Runö grew stronger every minute.

At one o'clock we sighted a steamer astern, coming out of the Sound and going S. She passed us several miles to eastward, very much disquieting the Ancient, who had never really trusted our compass after we had had its natural errors adjusted at Helsingfors.

"She'll be setting her course straight, and with her leaving us to west like that, we shall be passing Runö on the wrong side and getting among those shoals."

I had a hard job to persuade him that the steamer might have her course and we might have ours and both of us be right. I showed him the English mine-chart, with its swept channel for big ships far to eastward, close by Kynö Island, and explained that I wanted to keep well away from Kynö and its rocks and in the middle of the Gulf, so as to have a freer choice in case the wind should shift again. Also, the steamer's course would actually be longer than our own. He professed himself satisfied, but was not, until 6.15 in the afternoon, when, while he and the Cook were below and I was at the tiller, I saw something on the starboard bow that could not be a ship, that was . . . no . . . yes, actually was Runö Lighthouse. The lighthouse bore S.W. by W. I could not keep the triumph out of my voice as I shouted down the companion-way "Runö in sight"; but that unbelieving Ancient, when he came hurriedly up, stared over the port bow the moment his head was above the level of the deck, showing clearly what he had expected.

"Starboard bow," said I, "and pretty broad."

"By gum, you were right!" said the Ancient, and the quarrel ended. More serious matters were on hand. *Racundra* was moving much too fast. The men of Runö had been right about the coming gale, but had expected it a day too soon, and, even if we continued at the pace we were now going, racing in a bath of foam, we should, I calculated, be on the bar of Dvina about one in the morning. Now, leading lights are delightful things to steer by, and in most circumstances a well-lit harbour is easier for a stranger by night than by day. But the entrance to the

Dvina, child's play in ordinary weather, is a most tricky business with northerly winds. I quote from the *Baltic Pilot*: "On the shoals which are steep to, there is a heavy sea during northerly gales, and great difficulty would be experienced in clearing them." Further, there is a strong current across the entrance and also a current from the river, the total result being a thoroughly unpleasant bit of work for a little ship. On going out we had noticed an unlucky schooner which had failed to clear those shoals and had been flung ashore on the western side of the river mouth. Today, I knew that the current would be setting the other way, but I had no sort of wish to see *Racundra* swept on either side of the entrance to her home port at the end of her first cruise, and preferred to have daylight so as to be better able to judge the sea and the current and to decide in time whether to keep the sea or run in.

Accordingly, we brought *Racundra* to the wind and reefed her – reefed her relentlessly. It is a well-known fact that, while running before it, you do not feel the wind. It was not until we stopped there, a dozen miles off Runö, and brought *Racundra* up to face it, that we knew how strong the wind had grown. We took in both the deep reefs in the mainsail, turning it into a thing scarcely bigger than an afternoon tea cloth, and then stripped her of her mizen. We left the staysail standing, arguing that it would not do much pulling with the wind aft, and yet would perhaps hold a little wind in the troughs of the waves, even if the shortened mainsail should be wholly becalmed. Further, it would be of extreme usefulness if from some unpleasing accident we should happen to broach to. When all was done, I set a new course, S. by E., to bring us to the head of the Gulf, when we should sight the Riga lights a little on our port bow. That would give us something in hand for dealing with the current. Rough and ready navigation, you experts say, but it worked out admirably in practice. We then settled down for the night.

"Settled down" is perhaps not quite the phrase to use, for nothing could be very settled in such a sea as had got up. The Cook, for the first time on the whole voyage, was in a state of collapse, due partly to the fumes of the raw tobacco drying over the cabin lamp. The waves were so steep that the actual pitching of the ship, the lift and fall, not the rolling, was too much for the Primus gimbals. Nothing would stay on them. And *Racundra* seemed to be moving almost as fast as before we reefed her. The Ancient munched cheese, I swallowed raw eggs, and *Racundra* rushed along over a dark sea with breaking waves, the last of a stormy sunset in the west, on a green metallic patch of which we could just see the Runö Lighthouse and the topmost trees of the island. Behind us in the north were patches of starlight, which, as we watched them, were swept into blackness, and then everything went dark in a sudden torrent of rain. Then again were patches of starlight with huge clouds chasing small ones, and then a great mass that seemed suddenly to swell out till the whole sky was gone and the hailstones rattled on the decks.

It was a weird, exciting night, but not a happy one, for we knew that the worst was before us, that we were running for a lee-shore, that any mistakes would be disastrous, and that instead of comfortably getting our difficulties behind us, we were approaching them with every yard of *Racundra's* foaming path. I caught myself unashamedly regretting that we had tried this game so late in the autumn. "Especially during the autumn," the words of that pessimist *Baltic Pilot* glowed dully before me, and I asked myself, half angrily, why on earth I had not been content to fish for pike in England and to leave the Baltic to better men. And then, as always, *Racundra* comforted me. She ran so steadily, steered so easily, was so much less flustered than her "master and owner" when, glancing back, he saw the horizon, apparently only a few yards off, rise astern like a white-topped mountain, up and up and up, and nearer and nearer, till it seemed that it must overwhelm her in its majestic rush. But *Racundra* kept quietly on her path, rose as the huge wave reached her, dropped down its mighty back, and was running still while the horizon heaved itself again behind her for another effort.

Racundra, I say, comforted me. She seemed to have no doubt at all about what she could do or couldn't, and I found myself slowly coming to share her confidence. I sat with the tiller wedged between my left arm and my body, the hands thrust each into the opposite sleeve of my oilskins, on account of the exceeding cold. The Ancient crouched half-way down the companion-way and disliked talking. At regular intervals we changed places, and he who was off duty sheltered in the companion-way and tried to smoke the raw tobacco of the Werder lighthouse-keeper, a kindly gift, but a poor substitute for cut plug.

The lamps, of course, refused to burn, so we had the riding light in the companion-way and warmed our frozen hands on it when we left the tiller. As the night went on we began taking more and more frequent glances over the side with an electric torch on the foaming water, to see how fast *Racundra* was going. She was going much too fast. We began to feel a special hatred of the dark. It was as if someone had maliciously put the light out, and, with finger ready, was keeping it out for our annoyance. The night seemed unending. And then, at three o'clock, we saw unmistakably the glow of Riga lights on our port bow. That, of course, was just where they should have been, but we should have preferred to see them an hour or two later. Then they disappeared, leaving us to suppose that we were running into thick weather, when they would not be seen at all and we should be in worse case. Half an hour later we saw them again, and after that never wholly lost them. They are supposed to be visible twenty-five miles.

We held on, with redoubled impatience, watching the eastern sky for the faintest promise of light. Imperceptibly, even to us watchers, there came a difference in the darkness. The horizon on the port side was farther away. On that side one could actually see the waves, and the water, that had been black as the night except for its white splashes, was now the colour of a pewter mug.

Some time before that we had sighted the light-buoy ten miles out from Riga, and had had a pretty sharp demonstration of the strength of the current near the coast. We had, a little foolishly, made our course slightly more easterly on seeing the Riga high light. When we sighted the buoy, the Ancient was at the tiller. I asked him how it bore. "South by east." He steered straight for it, keeping the boat's nose on it whenever the waves let us see it. Before we reached it, I asked him again how it was bearing. He replied, "Southwest by west." It is what is known in these parts as a howling-buoy, and announces its opinion of its uncomfortable position by a long-drawn cry, between a groan and a whistle, as it lifts and falls in the waves. As we passed it after thus learning what sort of a current we had to contend with, this melancholy noise expressed our own feelings so perfectly that we had no need for words.

I decided to keep *Racundra* heading in such a way that a line between the howling-buoy's flashlight and the light from Riga should be to east of us, and to abandon the idea of getting in the moment we should find ourselves unable to keep on the right side of this imaginary line. After half an hour's rather anxious watching we were pretty well assured that we could do it, and when at last it grew light, just before we reached the second buoy, which is two miles out from the mouth of the river, we were confident of being able to stem the current and get in if it should not be reinforced by some particular malice of the waves. These, of course, were much steeper as we approached the bar, and we saw with some trepidation that three steamships were waiting outside, the pilot having evidently refused to come out during the night. Land was, of course, visible now alike to east and west. We could see Riga town and the white tower of the lighthouse, like a stick covered with hoar-frost in the grey, cold morning. Then there was the beacon on the eastern mole, and, as we came nearer, we saw the wrecked schooner that we had noticed on our way out and the furious white breakers storming the moles and charging angrily up the shores on either side of the entrance.

Still, just as we passed the second buoy, with its green light already blinking palely in the new daylight, we saw smoke in the mouth of the river and then the pilot tug coming out. We saw her and lost her, saw her and lost her in the waves as we approached. We passed her close by as she went to meet the steamers. She was sometimes literally half out of the water, and then, smashing down into a meeting wave, ceased to be a black tug, but became a single splash, higher than her own funnel-top, like the splash

"RACUNDRA" HAULED OUT.

CLYDE COOKER, FITTED 1923.

of a huge shell hitting the water horizontally. From her we got some sort of idea of what *Racundra* must be looking like, though that stout little ship, running with the wind, was making much better weather of it than the tug. *Racundra* was steering easily, and took only a few slight splashes of water over her stern (I do verily believe that there is nothing to beat the sharp-ended Scandinavian stern for running in a seaway) as she raced one huge wave after another towards the river mouth. One mountain after another came up behind her, seemed for a moment to carry her upon its grinding, foaming crest, and left her to be carried forward by the next, while she, good little thing, was doing her best herself.

And now we were already in the narrow lane of spar-buoys leading over the bar. Could she keep in it? Why, certainly she could, though the rollers were now disturbed by ugly, pyramidal angry waves that rushed across them as if to beat her from her course. But *Racundra*, demure, determined, shouldered them good-temperedly aside and held on. Almost before we knew it we were across the bar and in the entrance, watching with open mouths the tiny boats of the fishermen, labouring with their nets in the huge swell that came in from the sea. A northerly storm brings the fish to the Dvina, and next day the market was full of big salmon, so that the fishermen were well rewarded for their work. But *Racundra* is a lucky little ship. The night before, another boat, bigger than she, had tried to make the entrance, had failed, and been smashed to pieces in a few minutes on the eastern side of the river mouth. This we learnt from the Customs officials who, while congratulating us on getting in, now set about making our home-coming unpleasant.

Perhaps if we had been less tired and hungry their red-tape cobwebs, from which on going out we had been so happily excused, would not have annoyed us so much. And afterwards I felt inclined to forgive them, when I learnt that they had reason to believe that during the summer people had made use for smuggling of the privileges given by a yacht flag. Still, we were not smugglers, and, at the time, were very angry indeed. We had intended to sail straight up the river to be cleared in the Mühlgraben at the same Customs station where we had been cleared when outward bound. This, however, did not suit the officials at the Dvina mouth, and they behaved as if they had been told to make things difficult for little ships. They made us turn aside and anchor in the Winter Harbour. Then they nearly smashed our sides with a big Customs House tug. Then they made me row back to their office, and I was near being swamped in *Racundra's* cockleshell dinghy after *Racundra* herself had carried me so well. Then they said that, after all, we might proceed directly to the Yacht Club with an exciseman in charge on board, and wait there until they had sent an official from Riga. I rowed back very sulkily to the Winter Harbour, where we had breakfast, serving out a tot of rum to the elderly man who was now our gaoler.

Then, under the mainsail, we tacked out of the harbour and had a glorious run up the river, where were many sailing vessels, schooners, ketches and a fine barquentine, waiting for better weather and a favourable wind. We reached through the Mühlgraben past the little yellow Customs Office, past the now vacant berth where the *Baltabor* had been when we borrowed the lead, and carefully through the narrow channel into the Stint See. In smooth water and with the wind aft, *Racundra* slid easily homewards past the well-known landmarks, the old white boat high up on the eastern shore, the promontory of dark pine-trees on the western; and, at half past twelve on September 26th, rounded into the little sheltered harbour where, five weeks earlier, the dallying carpenters had been expelled from her and she had taken in stores before starting on her cruise.

Three hours later a Customs officer and a policeman arrived, and (crowning idiocy) they were the very same men who had passed us out, and had now had to walk the whole way from the Mühlgraben here, when I had myself proposed to anchor at their door and be cleared on the spot. They were no less full of wrath than I, and, as our papers were in order and we had drunk and eaten and smoked everything on board and so had nothing to declare, formalities were quickly over, the ensign hauled down, and *Racundra* was officially at home to lay up for the winter.

APPENDIX:
A DESCRIPTION
OF RACUNDRA

"RACUNDRA" is nine metres over all – something under thirty feet long. She is three and a half metres in beam – nearly twelve feet. She draws three feet six inches without her centreboard, and seven feet six inches when the centreboard is lowered. Her enormous beam is balanced by her shallowness, and though for a yacht it seems excessive, thoroughly justified itself in her comfort and stiffness. She has a staysail, mainsail and mizen, and for special occasions a storm staysail, a balloon staysail, a small squaresail (much too small), a trysail and a mizen staysail. She could easily carry a very much greater area of canvas, but, for convenience in single-handed sailing, she has no bowsprit, and the end of the mizen boom can be reached from the deck.

She is very heavily built and carries no inside ballast. Her centreboard is of oak. She has a three-and-a-half ton iron keel, so broad that she will rest comfortably upon it when taking the mud, and deep enough to enable us to do without the centreboard altogether except when squeezing her up against the wind. Give her a point or two free and a good wind and her drift, though more than that of a deep-keel yacht, is much less than that of the coasting schooners common in the Baltic. With the centreboard down she is extremely handy, and proved herself so by coming successfully through the narrow Nukke Channel with the wind in her face, a feat which the local vessels do not attempt.

But the chief glory of *Racundra* is her cabin. The local yachtsmen accustomed to the slim figures of racing boats, jeered at *Racundra's* beam and weight, but one and all, when they came aboard her ducked through the companion-way and stood up again inside that spacious cabin, agreed that there was something to be said for such a boat. And as for their wives, they said frankly that such a cabin made a boat worth having, and their own boats, which had seemed comfortable enough hitherto, turned into mere uncomfortable rabbit-hutches. *Racundra's* cabin is a place where a man can live and work as comfortably and twice as pleasantly as in

any room ashore. I lived in it for two months on end, and, if this were
a temperate climate, and the harbour were not a solid block of ice in
winter, so that all yachts are hauled out and kept in a shed for half the
year, I should be living in it still. Not only can one stand up in *Racundra's*
cabin, but one can walk about there, and that without interfering with
anyone who may be sitting at the writing-table, which is a yard square.
In the middle of the cabin is a folding table, four feet by three, supported
by the centreboard-case; and so broad is the floor that you can sit at that
table and never find the case in the way of your toes. The bunks are wider
than is usual, yet behind and above each bunk are two deep cupboards,
with between them a deep open space divided by a shelf, used on the port
side for books and on the starboard side for crockery. Under the bunks
is storage for bottles. Under the flooring on the wide flat keel is storage
for condensed milk and tinned food. Behind the bunks, between them
and the planking, below the cupboards and bookshelves, is further
storage room.

Racundra was designed as a boat in which it should be possible to
work, and, as a floating study or office, I think it would be difficult to
improve upon her. The writing-table is forward of the port bunk, and
a Lettish workman made me an admirable little three-legged stool, which,
when the ship is under way, stows under the table. Above and behind the
ample field of the table is a deep cupboard and a bookcase, of a height to
take the *Nautical Almanac*, the *Admiralty Pilots*, Dixon Kemp and Norie's
inevitable *Epitome* and *Tables*. Another long shelf is to be put up along the
bulkhead that divides the cabin from the forecastle. Under the shelf for
nautical books is a shallow drawer where I keep a set of pocket tools,
nails, screws and such things. Under the writing-table is a big chart
drawer, where I keep the charts immediately in use, writing and drawing
materials, parallel rulers, protractors, surveying compass, stopwatch and
other small gear. By the side of this is a long narrow drawer, used for odds
and ends, and underneath that is a special cupboard made to take my
portable typewriter.

On the starboard side, opposite the table, is space for a stove, which,
however, on this cruise we used for stowing spare mattresses. Behind it are
deep cupboards with low coamings to prevent things slipping. Here were
empty portmanteaux, seaboots, and a watertight box for photographic
material. The door into the forecastle is on this side, so that it is possible
to go through even when someone is sitting at the writing-table. In the

forecastle is one full-length comfortable bunk on the port side. On the starboard side there are big cupboards instead of a second bunk. These were used for ship's stores, such as blocks and carpenter's tools, shackles and the rest. A seat is fixed close by the mainmast, to a big central cupboard which is the full height of the forecastle from deck to floor, and was used for oilskins and clothes. In the forecastle we stowed warps, spare anchor, tins of kerosene, one of the water-barrels and the sails. This left small room for the Ancient Mariner, but, as he said, "There was room to lie and sleep, and room to sit and smoke, and what does any man want with more?" The main cabin is the general living room.

As you come out of the cabin into the companion-way, you find on either hand a cupboard from deck to floor. On the starboard side is a simple and efficient closet, and aft of that, under the deck, a big space used for all the engineering tools, lubricating oils and greases. On the port side is the galley, with room for three Primus stoves (I am fitting a Clyde cooker). One of the stoves is in heavy iron gimbals for use when under way. Behind this is a shelf and rack for cooking-things, and aft, under the deck, a second water-barrel. The engine, a heavy oil, hot-bulb Swedish engine, burning kerosene (we have no benzine in the ship), is under the self-draining steering-well. It is completely covered when not in use by a wooden case, contrived to provide steps up to the deck. The case takes to pieces, but can be fixed with absolute rigidity, so that people who have visited Racundra have asked on going away, what was the purpose of the reversing lever (at the side of the companion-way, within reach of the steering-well), never having suspected that we had an engine on board. For all the good we got of it during this first cruise we might just as well have had no engine, but next year I hope to take the engine seriously and learn the Open Sesame that will set it miraculously to work. The oil reservoir is in the extreme stern, and is filled from the deck. The companion-way can be completely covered in by a folding and sliding lid, over which we shall have a canvas cover. The raised trunking of the cabin is carried completely round companion, mizen mast and steering-well, so that there is plenty of room inside this coaming for a man to lie full length. In summer this would be a most desirable place to sleep, and even on this autumn cruise, during our days of fine weather, we put one of the spare mattresses there, and anyone who was not busy with something else reclined there, smoked, dozed, read or bothered the steersman with irrelevant conversation. The steering-well itself gives room for two people.

In front of it, immediately aft of the mizen mast, is the binnacle, and under the deck, between companion-way and steering-well, is a cupboard for riding light, binoculars, fog-horn, etc. The main sheet, mizen sheet, backstays and staysail sheets are all cleated within easy reach of the steersman, who can do everything but reef without leaving his place. Owing to the height of the narrow mainsail, inevitable in a ketch, the gaff tends to swing too far forward, so I have a vang, which also serves as a downhaul fastened to the peak, and cleated, when in use, close by the mizen mast.

RACUNDRA AFTER RANSOME

Following the completion of *Racundra's* third cruise in September 1924 the Ransomes left Latvia to live in the Lake District and *Racundra* was put up for sale to pay for their new home. She was purchased by Adlard Coles, at that time a young newly married yachting author, who was later to become head of a nautical publishing house bearing his name. The boat was advertised in *Yachting Monthly* magazine for £300 and after lengthy negotiations sold for £220. She was renamed *Annette II*, a condition of the purchase, as her new owner planned to write a book about her voyage to England. Coles and his wife sailed from Riga to Southwold in Suffolk from July 23rd to September 22nd 1925, via Sweden, Danish islands, Kiel Canal, Friesian islands and the North Sea, a distance of about 1350 nautical miles. *Close Hauled*, published by Seely, Service & Co Ltd in 1926, chronicles the trip. The boat was found by its new owner to be woefully under canvassed (she had a sail area of only 480 sq. ft.), and slow but able to withstand the atrocious weather they encountered in the North Sea. Of the engine Coles recorded: "Ran six miles. Six engineers to put it in order. Repair bill, six pounds."

In 1926 she was sold to Mr. R. P. Baker and reverted to her original name. Lloyds Register of Yachts records her as being owned by R. P. & Lt. H. B. Baker RN and registered in London. In 1927 she was fitted with an Ailsa Craig petrol motor, the new owner obviously giving up on the original 4 hp hot-bulb Swedish engine. In 1928 she became solely owned by R. P. Baker. A Mr. S. E. Palmer owned her from 1930 to 1933.

Racundra moved her Port of Registry to Southampton in 1933 and was owned jointly by Dr. E. T. Wright & Mrs. Alice E. Tyssen-Gee living not far from each other in Paddington and South Hampstead. Could this have been a repeat of the Master & Owner and the Cook relationship? She became solely owned by Dr. Wright in 1937, and was sold to R. J. St. Aubyn-Latham in 1938. He removed the Ailsa Craig and had her fitted with a four-cylinder Ford Universal petrol engine.

From 1939 to 1965, some 26 years, she was owned by J. M. Baldock, the Hampshire M. P. In 1952 Baldock converted her to Bermudan ketch rig, which increased her sail area to 600 sq. ft., and no doubt increased her performance considerably. At some time, possibly in the early 50s, her cabin had been extended to form a small "doghouse" over a part of the cockpit. In 1956 *Racundra* underwent a major refit at Mariners Boatyard, The Trippet, Bosham. Brian Fitzpatrick who carried out the work, wrote in December 2000:

"I first came across *Racundra* in a mud berth in Bosham circa1956. She had been laid up in this berth opposite the main village, known as Gosport side, for some years and was in a sorry state. The mast and gear had been stored in a boatyard on the Trippet known as 'Scovells', which yard I had bought soon after acquiring the larger yard named 'Mariners Boatyard' in 1952/3. I was approached by the then owner, a Mr. Baldock who lived in a small castle/country house some-where near Guildford (I think). He wanted to refit her into sailing order and install a new engine. We hauled her out into the undercover sheds to dry out and consider what to do. Among other things we found that the main stem post had rotted to the core. The planks were 'sprung back' and the whole stem removed down to the keel joint.

A new stem was fashioned by adze out of a grown oak crook, refitted and the planks refastened. All the plank seams were wide open and almost impossible to caulk, so we did the best we could and then splined them. The massive centre plate, built like a barn door with heavy iron straps, was jammed in its box and needed a lot of persuasion to remove. The external tackle needed to raise this very heavy item also needed renewing. The decks were replaced in large sections and then covered in the then new Epoxide resin and glass cloth. The whole interior was refurbished and new joinery made and fitted. A new Blake toilet installed and the galley fitted with a new paraffin stove. The heavy rack and pinion wheel steering gear to the Dutch barge type rudder was brought back to life again. Finally we fitted a new Coventry Victor flat twin diesel under the cockpit floor.

The masts and spars were scraped and revarnished and the rigging renewed and eventually, after repainting and varnishing, we launched her off into Bosham Quay. The old canvas sails were treated with red 'Cutch' before bending on. She looked very smart and ready for sea again. Unfortunately she somehow managed to hit the bar on one of her trial runs and drove the centreboard crashing up into its casing, causing damage and leaking. The owner took her round to 'Burnes' yard also in Bosham where they resorted to covering the underwater bottom with a rubber sheathing. 'Chunky Duff' of M.G. Duff, Chichester, was involved in the survey of damage and advised on repairs.

The stem was adzed out of a grown oak bend by Stan Bennett, a one-eyed boat-builder of Bosham. Henry Stoveld, boat-builder, rigger and waterman, ex Scovell's yard, caulked the seams. The interior joinery was largely made by a Les Turner, cabinetmaker, chair frame maker and machinist from 'Clubley and Rogers' of Southbourne. Francis Fitzpatrick of Bosham refurbished the sails & other canvas items, and the boat-builders, engineers, riggers and painters of Mariners Yard undertook the remainder of the work."

In 1965 she was sold to Tom Dickinson who had the troublesome centerboard removed and sold her to Adrian Haskins the following year. According to Lloyds Register his address was Tangier, Morocco. New Jeckells sails were purchased in 1967 & 1968. Her ownership was transferred to Quitos Ltd, No. 3 Governors Place, Gibraltar in 1974 and her homeport changed to Gibraltar.

In 1971 Mr. Haskins wrote to Mr. Glover, of Fareham:

40 SIDI BUJARI
TANGIER

Tel. 37397
November 12th. 1971
Dear Mr. Glover

I am glad you are so interested in 'RACUNDRA'. She is a lovely boat, & has personality, & evokes the admiration of all who see her, especially in full sail.

I am sorry to be so long in answering your letter, but my wife sent you a postcard, on sale in Morocco, taken unknown to me, just prior to her bi-annual visit to the slipway for anti-fouling etc. It gives you some idea of her present condition & rig, although the bowsprit is hardly discernable, the photograph having been taken dead for'ard.

She has been in my possession since 1965, & was bought by me in Gibraltar. She was on the slipway for over a month for various repairs & minor alterations, painting & varnishing. The masts were unstepped & all the rigging replaced. Mainmast 45', mizen 26'. She is now Bermudan rigged, with a sail area of over 500 sq. feet. Jib, foresail,

"RACUNDRA" IN TANGIER CONVERTED TO A BERMUDAN RIG.

"RACUNDRA" FITTING OUT IN TANGIER.

mainsail & mizen of Terylene, by Jeckells, 1968/9., the centreboard having been removed. A Coventry Victor Diesel engine 17HP, self-starter, was installed in 1959. A very solid & reliable job, which after an overhaul, is chiefly used for entry & exit from our marina.

She is in exceptionally good condition, as I have a Moroccan sailor, a very good chap, whose sole occupation has been to look after her in every way, under my supervision, for the last six years.

The hull is a sound as the day she was launched, & the only water in the bilge is via the propeller shaft bearing, which is very little. You will notice in the photograph, I now have railings surrounding the deck, which are well worthwhile, when I have my grandchildren & their friends aboard, on occasion, 14 in number.

The tiller has been replaced by a wheel, & the rudder actuated by SS cables. All stays & running rigging (halyards in part) are in stainless steel with Norseman terminals in SS, as well as shackles, although the majority are in bronze. All blocks are "Maine Marine", & ropes in nylon.

There is an excellent 'Head' in the foc's'le, completely enclosed by a mahogany surround, immediately aft the Samson post & chain locker.

EQUIPMENT. Lifeboat type compass, just aft the mizen, & for'ard of self-draining cockpit, barometer & clock as a pair. The Briggs & Gatehouse 'Homer' direction finder, & radio, Ferrograph depth sounder & 2 fire extinguishers are within the main hatchway visible from the cockpit, together with instrument panel, revolution counter, ampere meter, oil pressure gauge, & temperature of water in engine, there being an ancillary heat exchanger.

The exhaust pipes have been fitted with water jackets, to avoid the smell that usually follows those, which are lagged, the silencer being also water-cooled. Simpson Lawrence winch, 40lb. Danforth anchor & also Fisherman's with nylon rope, 70 fathoms of chain.

The cabin has had little structural alteration, & the revolving bar is a surprise & delight to everyone. All the upholstery is plastic, in blue to match the coaming between deck & cabin roof, in which brass opening scuttles have been fitted. The lockers & roof bearers are in oak, as originally made, the remainder of the boat being white. The deck, Admiralty grey/blue non-skid paint. The illumination is excellent three to cabin top & one over each end locker, i.e. one for chart & one for bar, one also, over mirror above door to foc'sle. 15 watts each.

She moves easily through the sea, & her hull design gives a very comfortable sail. She is quite handy, in spite of her beam, & as you have read in many sailing books, she is a first class heavy weather boat, & if she is maintained, as she now is, has a long life ahead. I sail every day when circumstances permit, & a force 4/5 is the sort of wind in which she revels. She was built in Riga, by O. Eggers, in 1922. 30 ft. long at waterline, she being a double ender, 36ft.overal, beam 11ft. 9ins. & 6ft. from sole to cabin top, draught 3ft. 9ins, TM 13 tons.

I am very glad to know the origin of her name, as I have so frequently been unable to give an answer. The previous owner, immediately prior to me, was a Mr. Dickinson, & before him, a Mr. Baldock, who I think was an M.P.

I am glad you are so devoted to the sea, & wish you the best of good luck, & many many years of happy sailing!

Yours truly

Adrian Haskins

During the ownership by Quitos Ltd in 1974 she must have deteriorated. In 1976 ocean sailor and adventurer Rod Pickering found her in a poor state in Morocco, purchased and restored her to her former glory. He crossed the Atlantic with her and arrived in Caracas in 1978. He spoke of her as being a "fine sea-going boat". He had intended to return to England via the West Indies. Later whilst sailing single-handed off the Venezuelan coast she hit a reef on Las Rogues and had to be abandoned. In a letter to Classic Boat magazine in June 1990, Humphrey Holland wrote:

"Some years ago a friend of mine, Rod Pickering, found her quietly decaying in a corner of Tangier Harbour. She had a crude doghouse over her main hatch and her centreboard and case had gone. She was rigged as a Bermudan ketch but her mizen was missing. After much wrangling we eventually obtained permission to take her out and, despite her depleted rig, she performed remarkably well. Rod bought her and refitted her in Estepona.

I had the good fortune to sail her a number of times and despite her great beam and minimal freeboard, she was a slippery and sea-kindly little boat.

About eleven years ago, *Racundra* was lost on Las Rogues north of Caracas. Her last cruise had encompassed Madeira, the Canaries, the Cap Verde Islands and the West Indies; it was an adventure to compare with the best of sea stories and I hope that Arthur Ransome would have approved."

Having lost his boat and his home, Rod Pickering said that he "felt like a snail without a shell." In June 1982 Rod and his cousin set sail in a catamaran from Martha's Vineyard, New England possibly bound for England. They were never seen again.

A final mystery survives: the very last Lloyds Register of Yachts in 1980 records *Racundra* as being owned by Rod Pickering as does its short-lived successor Debrett's Register of Yachts in its only two issues in 1983 & 1985. Perhaps she was "unwilling yet to accept the idea of a final resting place."

...UNWILLING YET TO ACCEPT THE IDEA OF A FINAL RESTING PLACE.

CHRONOLOGY

1884   Arthur Michell Ransome born on 18th January, Headingley, Leeds.

1897   Cyril Ransome, Arthur's father, dies; Arthur enters Rugby School.

1901   Enters Yorkshire College (now Leeds University) to read science.

1902   Leaves for London, works as errand boy for London publishers and becomes freelance writer.

1903   Meets W. G. Collingwood and his family.

1904   First book *The A.B.C of Physical Culture* published.

1907   First major book *Bohemia in London* published.

1909   13th March marries Ivy Constance Walker.

1910   9th May daughter Tabitha is born.

1912   *Oscar Wilde, a Critical Study* published.
       Sued for libel by Lord Alfred Douglas, won his case.

1913   Marriage falls apart, first visit to Russia.

1914   Leaves to work in Russia for *Daily News*.

1916   *Old Peter's Russian Tales* published.

1917   Meets Trotsky's secretary Evgenia Shelepina.

1919   Becomes special correspondent for *Manchester Guardian* and moves to Tallinn with Evgenia. Later they move to Lodenzee, Lahepe Bay about 40 miles from Tallinn.

1920   2nd July buys his first boat *Slug* on the beach at Tallinn.
       3rd July sails it 60 miles along the coast of Esthonia to Lahepe Bay.
       5th July writes to his old friend Barbara Collingwood with lots of questions about sailing.
       During the night of 7th – 8th July mainsail stolen.
       Wrote essay on the subject.

1921   In the spring, purchases second boat *Kittiwake*.
       13th April goes for trial sail.
       15th April meets Otto Eggers, boat designer.
       Possibility of *Racundra* looms.
       4th May dinghy, for *Kittiwake*, ordered from local undertaker arrives.
       11th May undertakes first major voyage of *Kittiwake* from Tallinn to Paldiski North.
       20th July sets sail on *Venera* (the pirate ship), lands on Hiiumaa and meets old man building large boat.

24th July walks to Heltermaa, visits Captain Konga on
Toledo of Leith.

Late July writes essay *On the Pirate Ship*.

August Ransomes move to Riga. Small sailing/fishing dinghy built
by Lettish boat builder.

Autumn, before a trip to England, signs the contract, with builder
of dinghy, for building of *Racundra*.

1922   January joins Cruising Association as foreign resident and appointed
Honorary Local Representative for Riga.

30th January article *The Ship and the Man* (taken from part of
On the Pirate Ship) published in the *Manchester Guardian*.

28th July, *Racundra* launched, unfinished.

20th August sets sail on *Racundra's* first cruise.

26th September returns to Riga and *Racundra* is laid up for the winter.

December trip to England, Ivy agrees to divorce, visits the Collingwoods
with diary/logbook of cruise. Encouraged to turn it into a book.

Christmas back in Riga and book well advanced.

1923   16th January final draft completed.

February fire destroys house at Kaiserwald, Riga.

Possibility of second book mentioned in a letter to his mother.

April, *Sailing in the Eastern Baltic* published in the *Cruising
Association Bulletin*.

July Racundra's First Cruise published.

18th July embarks on *Racundra's* second cruise, Riga to Finnish islands.

25th July to 21st August urgent meeting in London interrupts cruise.

6th September returned to Tallinn, *Racundra* is laid up for the winter.

1924   February, plans of *Racundra* published in *Cruising
Association Bulletin*.

March, visit to London to finalise divorce arrangements.

22nd March, elected a member of the Royal Cruising Club.

April, sail plans and lines of *Racundra* published in *Cruising
Association Bulletin*.

14th April divorce becomes absolute.

8th May Arthur and Evgenia marry at British Consulate Tallinn.

15th May to 22nd May, *Racundra* sailed back in Riga.

1st August to 10th September, *Racundra's* third cruise takes place,
from Riga on the river Lielupe to Jelgava.

Late September *Racundra* is laid up for the last time.

14th November Ransomes move to Low Ludderburn
in the Lake District.

1925   *Racundra* sold to Adlard Coles and her name changed to *Annette II*.

1928   Final trip to Russia for *Manchester Guardian*.

1929   24th March starts to write *Swallows and Amazons*.
19th June resigns from *Manchester Guardian* but still
works as a freelance.
December visits Cairo for *Manchester Guardian*.

1930   *Swallows and Amazons* published.

1931   *Swallowdale* published.
15th December joins the Cruising Association as a full member.

1932   *Peter Duck* published.

1933   *Winter Holiday* published.

1934   *Coot Club* published.

1935   *Nancy Blackett* purchased.

1936   *Pigeon Post* published.

1937   *We Didn't Mean to Go to Sea* published.

1938   *Selina King* launched.

1939   *Secret Water* published. Ivy dies.

1940   *The Big Six* published.

1941   *Missee Lee* published.

1943   *The Picts and the Martyrs* published.

1946   *Peter Duck* built.

1947   *Great Northern*? published.

1952   *Lottie Blossom* purchased.

1953   *Lottie Blossom II* built.

1954   30th August lays up *Lottie Lottie Blossom II*
for the last time and swallows the anchor.

1955   *Fishing* published.

1959   *Mainly About Fishing* published.

1965   Resigns from the Cruising Association.

1967   3rd June Arthur dies at Cheadle, Manchester.

1975   19th March Evgenia dies.

1976   *Autobiography* published.

1984   *The War of the Birds & the Beasts* published.

1988   *Coots in the North & other Stories* published.

2002   *Racundra's Third Cruise* published.

BIBLIOGRAPHY

Relevant Publications by Arthur Ransome

The ABC of Physical Culture, Henry Drane, 1904.

Bohemia in London, Chapman & Hall, 1907.

Oscar Wilde, Martin Seeker, 1912.

Old Peter's Russian Tales, T C & E C Jack, 1916.

Six Weeks in Russia, George Allen & Unwin, 1919.

The Soldier and the Death, J G Wilson 1920.

The Crisis in Russia, George Allen & Unwin, 1921.

Rod & Line, Cape, 1929.

Swallows and Amazons, Cape, 1930.

Swallowdale, Cape, 1931.

Peter Duck, Cape, 1932.

Winter Holiday, Cape, 1933.

Coot Club, Cape, 1934.

Pigeon Post, Cape, 1936.

We Didn't Mean to Go to Sea, Cape, 1937.

Secret Water, Cape, 1939.

The Big Six, Cape, 1940.

Missee Lee, Cape, 1941.

The Picts and the Martyrs, Cape, 1943.

Great Northern?, Cape, 1947.

Mainly About Fishing, A & C Black, 1959.

Autobiography, edited and with an introduction by Rupert Hart-Davis,
    Cape, 1976.

War of The Birds and the Beasts, Cape, 1984.

Coots in the North, Cape, 1988.

Signaling from Mars, a selection of letters edited and introduced
    by Hugh Brogan, Cape, 1997.

Racundra's Third Cruise, edited and compiled by Brian Hammett, Fernhurst 2002.

Other publications consulted

GC Davies, *The Swan and her Crew*, Warne, 1876.

EF Knight, *The Cruise of the Falcon*, Sampson Low, 1884.

EF Knight, *The Cruise of the Alerte*, 1890.

Adlard Coles, *Close Hauled*, Seely, Service, 1926.

The Cruising Association Handbook, 1928.

Hugh Shelley, *Arthur Ransome*, Bodley Head, 1960.

Taqui Altounyan, *In Aleppo Once*, John Murray, 1969.

Hugh Brogan, *The Life of Arthur Ransome*, Cape, 1984.

Christina Hardyment, *Arthur Ransome and Captain Flint's Trunk*,
    Cape, 1984.

Roger Wardale, *Arthur Ransome's Lakeland*, Dalesman Books, 1988.

Roger Wardale, *Arthur Ransome's East Anglia*,
    Poppyland Publishing, 1988.

Taqui Altounyan, *Chimes of a Wooden Bell*, I B Tauris, 1990.

Peter Hunt, *Approaching Arthur Ransome*, Cape, 1991.

Roger Wardale, *Nancy Blackett: Under Sail with Arthur Ransome*,
    Cape, 1991.

Jeremy Swift, *Arthur Ransome on Fishing*, Cape, 1994.

Ransome at Sea, Amazon Publications, 1995.

Roger Wardale, *In Search of Swallows and Amazons*, Sigma Leisure, 1996.

Ransome the Artist, Amazon Publications, 1998.

Roger Wardale, *Arthur Ransome and the World of Swallows & Amazons*, Great
    Northern Books, 2000.

Wayne G Hammond, *Arthur Ransome, a Bibliography*,
    Oak Knoll Press, 2000.

ACKNOWLEDGEMENTS

The research and publication of the present edition of *Racundra's First Cruise* would not have been possible without the help and assistance of a great many people. I particularly acknowledge the following:

Writers of books on Ransome, Hugh Brogan, Ransome's biographer, Wayne Hammond, Peter Hunt, Jeremy Swift, Roger Wardale, and particularly Christina Hardyment for her help and encouragement. I have drawn heavily on the work of these writers during the preparation of the preface.

Fay and Graham Cattell, members of the Cruising Association, for taking photographs of the area for me, allowing me to use them, and finding answers to my numerous queries from their friends in Latvia and Estonia. Arnis Berzins, the current Cruising Association Honorary Local Representative for Riga, for his continued support. Brian Fitzpatrick and Peter Glover for their information on Racundra after Ransome. Michael Howe, the Cruising Association's librarian, for allowing me access to their complete collection of Lloyds Register of Yachts. Essex Chronicle Series Ltd for the use of photograph of me on the flyleaf. Phyl Williams-Ellis of Fernhurst Books for passing on interesting leads from her myriad of contacts. Does she know everyone in the world?

Once again I owe an incredible debt to the Special Collections Department of the Brotherton Library, University of Leeds, and in particular the staff of that department for their help and assistance, and permission to use Ransome material and photographs for which they hold the copyright.

Ransome's Literary Executors for permission to embark on the reprint and use his previously published and unpublished work. Various members of the Arthur Ransome Society for their outstanding enthusiastic encouragement following the publication of *Racundra's Third Cruise*, with special thanks to Ted Alexander and Dave Sewart for the very considerable help and assistance they have given me throughout.

Finally, Tim Davison of Fernhurst Books for enthusiastically agreeing to the publication of another Ransome tome and enabling me to complete the project.

Brian Hammett,
Blackmore, Essex